Drafting Confidentiality Agreements

Second Edition

Related titles by Law Society Publishing

The Enterprise Act 2002
The New Law of Mergers, Monopolies and Cartels
Tim Frazer, Susan Hinchliffe and *Kyla George*
1 85328 896 9

The New Law of Insolvency
Insolvency Act 1986 to Enterprise Act 2002
Vernon Dennis and *Alexander Fox*
1 85328 812 8

Design Law
Successfully protecting and exploiting rights
Margaret Briffa and *Lee Gage*
1 85328 817 9

Technology Outsourcing
General Editor: *John Angel*
1 85328 832 2

Titles from Law Society Publishing can be ordered from all good legal
bookshops or direct from our distributors, Marston Book Services
(01235 465656 or e-mail law.society@marston.co.uk). For further
information or a catalogue, contact our editorial and marketing office at
publishing@lawsociety.org.uk.

DRAFTING CONFIDENTIALITY AGREEMENTS

Second Edition

Mark Anderson *Solicitor*
Principal, Anderson & Company

and

Simon Keevey-Kothari *Barrister*
Associate, Anderson & Company

The Law Society

ISBN 1 85328 937 X

Published in 2004 by the Law Society
113 Chancery Lane, London WC2A 1PL
Typeset by J&L Composition, Filey, North Yorkshire
Printed by TJ International Ltd, Padstow, Cornwall

Contents

Preface

The drafting of confidentiality agreements is a small, but important, subject. This book is intended as a practical guide to those agreements and to the 'law of confidence' which underpins them. It is in three parts: first, a brief discussion of how English law protects confidential information in a business context; second, a discussion of commercial practice in relation to confidentiality agreements, including a detailed commentary on the terms of such agreements; and finally, a selection of precedents for confidentiality agreements.

The content is based partly on the authors' experience of drafting and reviewing hundreds, if not thousands, of confidentiality agreements and clauses over the last 20 years for business clients, many of them technology-based companies and universities. A fair number of those agreements were prepared overseas, in the context of international transactions. Thanks are due to our clients for the opportunity to develop our knowledge of this global, niche subject.

This book attempts to be up to date in its discussion of English law as at May 2004.

Mark Anderson
Shillingford
May 2004
www.andersonsolicitors.com

Table of cases

Table of statutes and statutory instruments

Law

CHAPTER 1

The law relating to confidentiality

INTRODUCTION

The aim of this book, as the title suggests, is to act as a guide in relation to the drafting of confidentiality agreements, which generally rely on the use of the law of confidence as a means of protecting confidential information in a commercial setting.

The law relating to the protection of confidential information, traditionally known as the law of confidence, is a large subject that covers many types of confidential information and factual circumstances. The protection of commercial information is just one part of the overall subject, but it will be the main focus of this book. Thus, for example, the details of the case law dealing with personal privacy and state secrets are matters outside the remit of this book and will only be dealt with in passing. For an in-depth understanding of the whole area of the law relating to breach of confidence, readers should consult the established texts in this area.

Confidential information, in the context of this text, will mean information relating to a business, which is of value due to not being generally known and which gives that business a competitive edge over its rivals. Businesses will generally regard any information in their possession that gives them any sort of competitive advantage as confidential. Such confidential information may commonly, for example, comprise details of manufacturing processes, chemical formulae or sales lists. It should, however, be made clear that the law of confidence obviously applies equally to any kind of information, not just the commercially valuable, provided it has the necessary quality of confidence.

CONFIDENTIALITY OBLIGATIONS

Legal basis

As will be discussed later, the origins of the law of confidence are in equity and contract. The vast majority of persons owe an obligation of confidence to someone – all employees have a duty of confidence or fidelity to their employers, consultants owe a duty to their clients, doctors have a duty of confidence in respect of their patients, and solicitors are bound by a duty of confidence to their clients. While this text intends to deal mainly with the contractual basis of obligations of confidence, it will also touch upon the other bases, for the sake of completeness.

Many different kinds of information may be imparted in confidence. English law, unlike other legal systems, does not distinguish between or attempt to classify fully the various types of information that may be protected by the law relating to confidentiality. Confidential information is not limited to the written or printed word and an image can also comprise confidential information. For example, in *Douglas* v. *Hello! Ltd* [2001] FSR 732, at the wedding of the actors Michael Douglas and Catherine Zeta-Jones a person unknown to the wedding party took photographs without authorisation. These photographs were to be published by the defendant in its magazine but an interim injunction was obtained (and the claimants subsequently won their action for breach of confidence against *Hello!* magazine, despite adjudications on some aspects of the claims in the defendants' favour, see *Douglas and others* v. *Hello! Ltd and others* (No. 3) [2003] EWHC 786 (Ch)).

Another celebrity confidential information/privacy case, the fashion model Naomi Campbell's victory over the *Daily Mirror* newspaper, was the subject of a recent House of Lords decision ([2004] UKHL 22). The case involved pictures, published by the *Daily Mirror*, of Miss Campbell leaving a narcotics anonymous treatment centre. Miss Campbell brought her case under the law of confidence, and the five law lords agreed that the law of confidence had now developed into a law that would provide 'a remedy for the unjustified publication of personal information' (per Lord Hoffmann).

Statutory recognition

There is no statutory codification of the law of confidence, although the Law Commission once proposed such a statute, and even prepared a draft code. A copy of the draft Bill is included as an appendix to Gurry, *Breach of Confidence*, Clarendon Press, 1984.

However, there is some statutory recognition of the law of confidence. For example, the Copyright, Designs and Patents Act 1988, s.171(1) states that:

> Nothing in this Part [the part of the Act dealing with copyright law] affects . . . the operation of any rule of equity in relation to breaches of trust or confidence.

It should also be noted that, in relation to state secrets, the Official Secrets Act 1989 details a number of offences relating to the disclosure of confidential information to unauthorised persons.

INTELLECTUAL PROPERTY RIGHTS

As far as technological ideas are concerned, confidentiality cannot really play any sort of long-term role unless the information can be put to commercial use without at the same time coming into the public domain. If commercial use of a product reveals the information in question, it will lose its quality of confidence, although limited protection under the 'springboard doctrine' (discussed in Chapter 2) may be available.

Patents

If the information is to be patentable, it must not (subject to some very limited exceptions) have been publicly disclosed prior to filing the patent application; thus, any disclosures of the invention prior to filing should be made in confidence so as not to prejudice the patent application.

There may, however, be circumstances in which the inventor may decide to keep his invention secret in preference to obtaining a patent. Patenting involves public disclosure of the invention and usually gives a maximum of 20 years' protection. Obviously, the course of action to be taken depends partly on whether the actual information can be kept secret, and if so, for how long.

Copyright

As regards copyright, it is established that copyright does not protect ideas as such, but only the expression of ideas. The law of confidence, however, can and does protect ideas, but only until such time as those ideas are published in some manner. Thus, a proposal for a book on drafting confidentiality agreements might be disclosed to a publisher in confidence, in which case unauthorised use of that proposal by the publisher would be a breach of confidence. However, once the book were published, the proposal would lose its 'necessary quality of confidence'.

Conversely, the idea of making such a book available would not be protected by copyright (unless there were direct copying of the proposal document). Anyone could write a competing book and, as long as it did not copy or adapt a substantial part of the first book's text, it would be unlikely to be an infringement of the first book's copyright.

CONFIDENTIALITY BEFORE IP RIGHTS ARISE

A right of action for breach of confidence will often underpin, and in many cases comes into play before, a more formal intellectual property right. An idea for any sort of novel process will not have any copyright protection until it is translated into a tangible form. But if an idea is discussed secretly with another person who then uses the idea to, for example, develop a new manufacturing process using the same idea, then there may be an actionable breach of confidence.

In the arena of patentable inventions, the idea for a new invention may be protected by the law of confidence before the stage of a working patentable model is reached.

Whereas other rights such as copyright and patents are particularly useful when the subject matter is made public by the owner of the material, the law of breach of confidence gives protection to information that has not yet been made public knowledge. This is in a way the main purpose of the law of confidence, and its most useful feature therefore is that, in appropriate cases, an injunction can be obtained preventing an anticipated wrongful release or use of the information.

CONFIDENTIAL INFORMATION AS PROPERTY

Some commentators have espoused the view that confidential information should be considered a form of property. While confidential information may have a substantial economic value, the accepted view is that it is not property – confidential information is not recognised as property for the purpose of the Theft Acts, although it is possible to steal the actual physical medium upon which the information is stored (see *Oxford* v. *Moss* (1978) 68 Cr App R 183).

In 1997, a Law Commission paper entitled *Legislating the Criminal Code: Misuse of Trade Secrets* (LCCP No. 150 (HMSO) 1997) recommended that the unauthorised use or disclosure of a secret be a criminal offence. At the present time, however, the basis for an action for breach of confidence is still in the realms of contract or equity.

A BRIEF HISTORY OF THE LAW OF CONFIDENCE

The modern law of confidence began to fall into place in the middle of the nineteenth century with *Prince Albert* v. *Strange* (1849) 2 De G & Sm 652, and *Morison* v. *Moat* (1851) 9 Hare 241, which are discussed below. In both cases injunctions were granted against indirect recipients of confidential information.

The equitable basis of the law of confidence 'is ancient', according to Megarry J in *Coco* v. *AN Clark (Engineers) Ltd* [1969] RPC 41. In both *Prince Albert* v. *Strange* and *Morison* v. *Moat*, the courts identified an equitable jurisdiction for breach of confidence actions, which would operate separately from any contractual relationship between the parties. In both of these cases, a number of causes of action were advanced to justify the protection of confidential information, including breach of trust and contract, but in both cases the courts also identified breach of confidence as a separate cause of action.

Prince Albert v. *Strange* involved an action brought by the husband of Queen Victoria. The royal couple had been in the habit of privately making drawings and etchings intended for their own private entertainment. A number of these drawings were sent to be printed professionally. While at the printers, someone surreptitiously made some additional prints from the etchings, which then came into the hands of the defendant who intended to display them for profit at a public exhibition. The action against Strange was therefore not an action based on a contract, as the royal couple had not entered into any contract with him. The House of Lords took the view that the action arose as an aspect of the claimant's proprietary rights in the drawings, but pointed out that the action was equally sustainable on grounds of equity, confidence and contract law.

The other early case in this area is *Morison* v. *Moat*, which involved as parties two business partners who developed a commercial medicine. The partnership ended and there was then a dispute involving one of the partners who originally devised the recipe and the son of the other partner, whose father had told him the recipe. It was held to be a 'breach of faith' and of contract by the partner, Moat, to tell his son of the secret who, therefore, could not claim title to the recipe. While the term 'breach of confidence' was not used at this stage, it was clear that the breach of faith was actionable independent of the existence of a contract, as there was no contractual relationship between the parties, and the claimant's claim was that the defendant was making improper use of information gained during the period of the partnership. The claimant sought an injunction. The injunction was granted, with the court accepting that the basis of the action was not totally clear, but that it may well have been based on trust or confidence creating an obligation on the defendant's conscience not to breach that confidence.

In the late-nineteenth-century case of *Robb* v. *Green* [1895] 2 QB 315 the defendant secretly copied a customer list from his employer. The Court of Appeal found that this conduct was in breach of an implied contractual term, but the basis of that term was the good faith that must exist between employer and employee.

The ability of the court to act independently in equity in the absence of express or implied contractual obligations of confidentiality was further confirmed in a number of key twentieth-century decisions: according to Lord Greene MR in *Saltman Engineering* v. *Campbell Engineering* (1948) 65 RPC 203, CA 'if a defendant is proved to have used confidential information directly or indirectly obtained from a claimant without the consent, express or implied, of the claimant, he will be guilty of an infringement of the claimant's rights'. He went on to say that the obligation to respect confidence is not limited to cases where the parties are in a contractual relationship. The judgment of the Court of Appeal in *Seager* v. *Copydex* [1967] RPC 349 confirmed that the court will act independently of the law of contract. The claimant, during preliminary negotiations with the defendants, revealed to them secret information about a carpet grip of their own which apparently made use of the claimant's information. There was no contract between the parties. In his judgment, Lord Denning MR stated that the law on this subject does not depend on any implied contract, but on the broad principle of equity that he who receives information in confidence shall not take unfair advantage of it.

In the mid-twentieth century, it became clear that this area of law was useful to protect intellectual property, especially during the development stages of a product, before protection could be obtained by virtue of other legal rights. Starting with *Saltman* v. *Campbell*, referred to above, the courts have recognised a wider equitable jurisdiction, based on good faith rather than property or contract, and this approach is now reasonably established within the judiciary. In that case, the claimant owned the copyright in drawings of tools for use in the manufacture of leather punches. The defendant was given the drawings and instructed to make the tools. After completing the order, the defendant retained the drawings and made use of them for its own purposes. In finding for the claimant, the court held that there was an implied condition that the defendant should treat the drawings as confidential, not make other use of them and should deliver up the drawings with the tools made pursuant to the agreement. It was held, further, that the information, to be confidential, must 'have the necessary quality of confidence about it' . . . 'it must not be something which is public property and public knowledge'.

The much more recent *Attorney-General* v. *Guardian Newspapers Ltd* [1988] 3 All ER 567 case, known as *Spycatcher*, also made it clear that confidentiality obligations may arise independently of any contractual relationship, as an equitable principle.

Given that the equitable nature of an action for breach of confidence is therefore at its very core, it is important to be aware that anyone considering bringing such an action should generally not him or herself have acted in an unconscionable manner.

The elements which will normally be required for a breach of confidence action to succeed are set out in the case of *Coco* v. *Clark* by Megarry J, and form the structure of Chapter 2 of this book.

CONFIDENTIALITY OBLIGATIONS BASED IN CONTRACT

It is always advisable to protect confidential information by entering into written confidentiality obligations prior to disclosing it to another party – indeed the drafting of such obligations is the main theme of this book. Such confidentiality obligations may be set down in the form of a confidentiality agreement, or as a discrete clause in a larger agreement, such as an employment contract.

It should be noted, however, that even express contractual terms may be narrowed in scope by the court, or rendered unenforceable, if publication of the information is held to be in the public interest (as in the case of *Hubbard* v. *Vosper* [1972] 2 QB 84); this aspect of the law of confidence will be dealt with briefly in Chapter 2.

Express contractual terms can also be held to be void or unenforceable if they are drawn too widely and result in an unlawful restraint on the actions of one of the parties to the agreement (see Chapter 2). This type of situation can arise for example in relation to employees once they leave their employment (see Chapter 4 for further details).

Conversely, in certain circumstances the courts may imply a contractual term in the absence of an express obligation to respect confidentiality. The case law in this area also shows that it is not unusual for the court to identify both equitable and contractual obligations based on the same set of facts.

The following chapter will discuss the main requirements of a breach of confidence action.

CHAPTER 2

Essential features of the law

INTRODUCTION

The usual reason for entering into a confidentiality agreement is in order to protect information that the disclosing party *considers* to be confidential. This chapter aims to provide guidance as to how one can be sure that one's information will be considered confidential by an English court, and can thus be afforded full protection by the confidentiality agreement.

The basic ingredients of a successful action for breach of confidence are laid out by Megarry J in *Coco* v. *AN Clark (Engineers) Ltd* [1969] RPC 41, a case where the confidential information in question was related to the development of a new type of moped engine.

The three elements that will normally be required for an actionable breach of confidence, as set out by Megarry J, are that:

1. The information must have the 'necessary quality of confidence about it'.
2. The information must have been imparted in circumstances where the recipient ought reasonably to have known that the information had been imparted in confidence.
3. There must be unauthorised use or disclosure of that information to the detriment of the party communicating it.

Megarry J's three elements serve as a useful starting point for analysis, and are dealt with in turn in the following paragraphs.

THE NECESSARY QUALITY OF CONFIDENCE

Confidential information must 'have the necessary quality of confidence about it'. There does not, however, seem to be a positive definition of what exactly constitutes confidential information in the case law; the courts have rather proposed a negative definition – e.g., in *Saltman*, Lord Greene stated that confidential information 'must *not* be something which is public property and public knowledge' (see *Saltman Engineering Co Ltd* v. *Campbell Engineering Co Ltd* [1963] 3 All ER 413).

In order to ascertain whether or not information has the 'necessary quality of confidence about it', Megarry J in *Thomas Marshall (Exports) Ltd* v. *Guinle* [1979] 1 Ch 227 stated that there are four elements to be considered:

1. The owner must believe that disclosure of the information would be injurious to him or of advantage to his clients.
2. The owner must believe the information is confidential or secret.
3. The above two beliefs must be reasonable.
4. Trade practice must be taken into account when considering the information.

In *Coco* v. *Clark*, Megarry J stated that no matter how confidential the circumstances of communication were, there could be no breach of confidence in revealing to others something which had already become common knowledge. Therefore, generally, once information is in the public domain it is no longer confidential.

An objective test should be applied to determine whether information is really confidential. Simply marking a document with the words 'Private & Confidential' is not enough if the contents lie within the public domain (*Dalrymple's Application* [1957] RPC 449).

Megarry J's suggestion, in *Thomas Marshall*, that common trade practice should be taken into account when deciding whether a certain type of information will be regarded as confidential, was taken up in *IBCOS Computers Ltd* v. *Barclays Mercantile Highland Finance Ltd* [1994] FSR 275. Jacob J said that the source code for a computer program was confidential since it was not usually given to clients by software developers who regarded it as confidential. Even if a source code is made available to a client under a licence agreement, the licence will almost certainly contain terms imposing an obligation of confidence on the licensee in respect of the source code.

The concept of the public domain

The boundary of what is and is not protectable by way of confidentiality obligations is determined by the public domain, as is apparent from *Saltman*, where 'public property and public knowledge' were used to mark the boundary.

In relation to what actually is meant by public property and public knowledge, the Court of Appeal in *Woodward* v. *Hutchins* [1977] 2 All ER 751 held that the facts of various extramarital activities of the singer Tom Jones and other celebrities fell within the public domain since the acts that were the subject of the information had been carried out in public places.

Whether information is in the public domain depends on whether the information has been made freely available to the public. The test is whether such a degree of secrecy exists that, except by improper means, a member of the public would have difficulty in acquiring the information.

In order to afford protection under the law of confidence, the information does not have to be particularly special in any way, and a unique compilation of information in the public domain can, when taken as a whole, be regarded as confidential. What makes such information worth protecting by confidence is the fact that time and effort has been expended in gathering, selecting and arranging the information. In other words, a competitor should not be permitted to take a short cut by using information belonging to someone else; he should have to go through a similar process and spend time and energy to discover the information for himself. As Megarry J observed in *Coco* v. *Clark*:

> Novelty depends upon the thing itself, and not upon the quality of its constituent parts ... To endow such information with the necessary quality of confidence, some product of the human brain, whether it be termed skill, originality or ingenuity, must have been applied to its creation.
> (*Coco* v. *AN Clark Engineers Ltd* [1969] RPC at p. 47)

In *Ocular Sciences Ltd* v. *Aspect Vision Care Ltd* [1997] RPC 289, it was suggested that confidentiality would not reside in a substantial collection of data all of which was in the public domain, in this case a list of features of contact lenses, because even though it had presumably required time and effort to compile, it had required no particular skill. In *Schering Chemicals* v. *Falkman* [1981] 2 All ER 321, the information at issue was only available to any member of the public who was prepared to undertake a lengthy and painstaking trawl through the scientific literature. The defendant had not made such a search, and was thus held to have breached confidentiality obligations.

As stated above, the information in question may be a compilation of various pieces of information. Where such a compilation comprises a mixture of confidential information and matter already in the public domain, in order for protection to be afforded under the law of confidence it is up to the claimant in any action to clearly identify what is confidential and what is not. Where the information can actually be separated out and the confidential information identified, then the claimant must do that (see *Gadget Shop Ltd* v. *Bug.Com Ltd* [2001] FSR 383, where the claimant had not adequately separated confidential from non-confidential material).

As to what is exactly entailed in coming into the public domain, according to Scott J in one of the *Spycatcher* cases – *Attorney-General* v. *Guardian Newspapers Ltd* [1988] 3 All ER 567 – the answer will depend upon the circumstances of the case, and the court will often take a different view depending on whether it is dealing with commercial information, government information or personal information.

Certain types of publication do have the effect of putting information into the public domain. When a patent is applied for, details of the patent are published on the Patents Register, and are available for public inspection 18 months after the priority date. Such publication will destroy confidentiality in the subject matter, as in *Mustad* v. *Alcock and Dosen* [1964] 1 WLR 109, a case relating to anglers' fish-hooks.

On the other hand, in *Cranleigh Precision Engineering* v. *Bryant* [1965] 1 WLR 1293, the defendant, a director of the claimant, learned of a patent that affected the claimant's design of above-ground swimming pools, a fact he withheld from the claimant. He purchased the patent and then set up a competing business. He was found liable for breach of confidence despite his argument that the information contained in the patent specification was in the public domain. In *Cranleigh*, the information covered by the patent had not been published by the claimant, as was the case in *Mustad*. Rather, the defendant had used confidential information which had been available to him while serving as a director of the company to take advantage of the patent himself.

Trade secrets

In the context of this book, the information in question will usually (but not always) be a 'trade secret' related to business, commercial or industrial activity. As to what is meant by trade secret, a (rather simplistic) test was suggested by Lord Parker in *Herbert Morris Ltd* v. *Saxelby* [1916] 1 AC 688: 'if the information is of such detail that it cannot be carried in one's head then it is a trade secret, but if it is just some kind of easily remembered general method then it will not qualify as a trade secret'.

The classification of some forms of confidential information as trade secrets is important because the protection afforded by the law may sometimes depend upon it. The distinction between trade secrets and other classes of confidential information is particularly important in the context of employees' duties of confidentiality, discussed in Chapter 4. Unfortunately, there is no satisfactory legal definition of the term. While it is clear that a secret industrial process containing an inventive step is capable of being a trade secret, the position is less predictable in terms of confidential price lists, databases containing customer names and addresses and clients' accounts. Lord Parker's test of what can be remembered by an ex-employee does not necessarily help, as many new inventions may easily be remembered. Neither would it be realistic to limit trade secrets to inventions that are potentially patentable. Drawings, quotations, price costing and business strategies have all been considered to rank as trade secrets (*PSM International plc* v. *Whitehouse & Willenhall Automation Ltd* [1992] FSR 489). On the other hand, the mere application of obvious principles to an industrial process does not in itself give rise to a trade secret.

It is also unlikely that the bundling together of a number of well-known or obvious features would amount to a trade secret. In *Cantor Fitzgerald International* v. *Tradition (UK) Ltd* [2000] RPC 95, it was held that a technique used for testing computer software which was readily derivable by a skilled man from public sources is not a trade secret, as it was considered to be merely a useful technique which a technician may use.

Trade secrets are discussed further in Chapter 4.

Reverse engineering

Placing a product on the market will not in itself destroy the confidentiality of the relevant information, even though the information may be derived by reverse engineering of the product or by other analysis of it, if it would require substantial work to acquire such information, as in *Terrapin* v. *Builders Supply Co (Hayes) Ltd* [1967] RPC 375. In *Terrapin*, the claimants designed and marketed a novel type of portable building, which the defendants manufactured on their behalf. The defendants, making use of confidential information from the claimants, manufactured and marketed very similar buildings once their contract with the claimants had expired. The defendants argued that by publishing detailed brochures and putting their buildings on the market so that a purchaser might analyse them, the claimants had destroyed any confidentiality. This argument was rejected. The court found that a member of the public, without the benefit of the confidential information, would have had to employ considerable effort in order to analyse the buildings in this way. The information was not, therefore, accessible to the public.

On the other hand, it was more recently held that encrypted information in a commercially available computer program did not have the necessary quality of confidence about it: *Mars UK Ltd* v. *Teknowledge Ltd* [2000] FSR 138; any purchaser with the skills to de-encrypt the program would have access to the information. The mere fact that the information was encrypted did not make it confidential. Jacob J stated that the message that comes across by encrypting information is that the owner does not want another person to gain access to it. Without more, encrypting on its own cannot impose an obligation of confidence.

The springboard doctrine

While in most cases publication of confidential information generally removes the obligation of confidence, a person under an obligation of confidence prior to publication can still be held to be under an obligation of confidence for a further period after publication. A party who receives information under a confidentiality agreement therefore needs to bear this in mind, and not assume they are freed from their obligations once the disclosing party has made the subject matter public.

As Roxburgh J stated in *Terrapin*:

> a person who has obtained information in confidence is not allowed to use it as a springboard for activities detrimental to [the owner] and springboard it remains even when all the features have been published . . .
>
> (*Terrapin* v. *Builders Supply Co (Hayes) Ltd* [1967] RPC at p. 392)

The person who was under an obligation of confidence is therefore not allowed to use it as a springboard from which to launch his own activities if that would result in harm to the person to whom the obligation was owed. The basic idea behind the springboard doctrine is to remove any unfair advantage that a recipient might derive from the receipt of confidential information which later becomes public, by trying to bring the recipient back to a common starting point with parties who had not received the information earlier.

It is probably best to illustrate the doctrine by examining the two main cases – *Terrapin*, mentioned above, and *Cranleigh Precision Engineering Ltd* v. *Bryant* [1964] 3 All ER 289.

In *Terrapin*, the claimants designed portable buildings and engaged the defendants to construct them. To this end, the claimants provided confidential design specifications to the defendants. Once the arrangement between the parties ended, the defendants started producing buildings which were very similar in design to the claimants'. Although the information was now no longer confidential, as the structure of the buildings could be examined by anybody, Roxburgh J granted an injunction to ensure that the defendants would not be in a position where they could use information gained in confidence from the claimants to compete with the claimants. In *Terrapin*, the springboard doctrine was therefore used to deprive the defendant of the unfair advantage he would have had as a result of his breach of confidence.

In *Cranleigh*, the defendant, a director of the claimant, learned of a patent which affected the claimant's design of above-ground swimming pools, and withheld this finding from the claimant. The defendant purchased the patent and then set up a competing business, based on the patent and information obtained while serving as a director of the claimant. The claimant applied for an injunction to prevent the defendant from using its information. The injunction was granted – the defendant was thus found liable for breach of confidence despite his argument that the information contained in the patent specification was in the public domain. He was prevented from using the information gained while an employee of the claimant (without which he would not have seen the importance of the patent he purchased) as a springboard in establishing his new business.

Springboard relief will not, however, be granted simply because the defendant has made an unauthorised use of the claimant's confidential information. The defendant must have gained an unfair competitive advantage over the claimant which still exists at the time of the action.

If the information is published by the confider, then the springboard issue does not arise, since no continuing obligation of confidence remains for any party including the original recipient. But where the confidential information is published by a third party, the recipient may well remain under a continuing obligation of confidence, especially if he came across the information because of his special relationship with the claimant, as was the case in *Cranleigh*.

How long should the obligation not to use the information last, under the springboard doctrine? In commercial situations, the recipient's obligation should be limited in time (*Potters-Ballotini* v. *Weston-Baker* [1977] RPC 202, CA). It has further been suggested that the restraint should also last only so long as the recipient would continue to have an unfair advantage (see *Roger Bullivant* v. *Ellis* [1987] FSR 172).

INFORMATION IMPARTED IN CONFIDENCE

The second element in *Coco* is that the information must have been 'imparted in circumstances where the recipient ought reasonably to have known that the information had been imparted in confidence' – which will ultimately hinge on the nature of the relationship between the parties.

How the obligation can arise

In commercial situations, the parties will often be in a contractual relationship, and may have entered into a separate confidentiality agreement (along the lines of those described in this book), or there may be an express contractual term in a main contract between the parties which establishes a relationship of confidence. The court may also in some cases imply such a term, e.g., in an employment contract.

While the main purpose of this text is not to deal with implied confidentiality provisions, but rather express provisions set out in confidentiality agreements, an understanding of how the courts have implied obligations of confidentiality is still useful by way of showing the overall legal context in which confidentiality agreements may be interpreted.

From the point of view of how to determine whether information was communicated in circumstances which gave rise to an obligation of confidence, a common test recognised by the courts is to ask whether the information was given for a specified or permitted purpose only. Indeed, readers will see in later chapters that a 'permitted purpose' is generally a defined term in most confidentiality agreements. A typical permitted purpose might be the evaluation of a particular piece of technology or business proposal, in order to decide whether to negotiate a commercial agreement with the provider.

In *Saltman*, it was held that the defendants had an equitable obligation to keep drawings confidential because they knew that they had been given to them for a permitted purpose only, in this case for manufacture of the tools for the claimant's use and not the defendant's use (similar reasoning can be found in *Ackroyds* v. *Islington Plastics* [1962] RPC 97). The permitted purpose test is generally seen as an objective one, and it is not necessary for the defendant actually to know that the confidential information was imparted for a particular purpose.

However, in *Carflow Products (UK)* v. *Linwood Securities (Birmingham) Ltd* [1996] FSR 424, Jacob J held that with respect to the equitable, as opposed to contractual, obligation of confidence, a subjective test is more appropriate – i.e., what obligations the parties thought they were imposing or accepting, and not what a reasonable man would think they were doing. In *Carflow*, the claimants produced a steering-wheel lock for which they had a registered design. The defendants showed a similarly designed prototype of the lock to a buyer for a chain of stores some time before the claimants' lock went on sale. Applying a subjective test, Jacob J did not believe that either the buyer or the defendants thought that the information had been given in confidence at the time the plaintiff disclosed the information to the defendant. Although Jacob J thought the subjective test most appropriate to the circumstances, he also found that an objective test would have a similar result.

It should however be noted that Jacob J did actually later make use of the reasonable man's objectivity in *Mars* v. *Teknowledge*, in assessing whether the de-encryption of the claimant's commercially available software could be said to be a breach of confidence.

UNAUTHORISED USE OR DISCLOSURE

The third element in *Coco* is that there must be unauthorised use of the confidential information, and that use must be to the detriment of the party communicating it. Although Megarry J's third element in *Coco* indicated that for a breach to occur the unauthorised use must include 'detriment' to the confider, there is by no means consensus on this point. In practice, it is unlikely that a claimant will bring an action for breach of confidence unless he expects to suffer, or has already suffered, from the defendant's unauthorised use or disclosure. In commercial confidentiality scenarios, disclosure of the information will almost always be detrimental, and therefore will not be dealt with in any detail in this section.

Parties to confidentiality agreements often think that the agreement can only be breached by disclosure of the confidential information. It is important to remember however that breach can be either by *use* or *disclosure*. Three elements need to be shown:

(a) that the recipient has used or disclosed the confidential information;

(b) that the information was obtained from the confider directly or indirectly; and

(c) that the use or disclosure went beyond the purpose for which the information was confided.

In *Saltman*, Greene MR stated:

> If a defendant is proved to have used confidential information, directly or indirectly, obtained from the claimant without the consent, express or implied, of the claimant he will be guilty of infringement of the claimant's rights.
> (*Saltman Engineering* v. *Campbell Engineering* (1948) 65 RPC at p. 213)

In *Saltman*, the defendants were found to have breached the relationship of confidence because they used the drawings to make tools and punches on their own behalf as opposed to manufacturing them on the claimant's behalf. Their use therefore went beyond that authorised by the claimants.

In *Thomas Marshall*, where a subjective element played a part, Sir Robert Megarry VC examined the relationship between use and disclosure. The claimant employed the defendant as a managing director. There was an express clause in the defendant's contract not to 'disclose' during or after employment any confidential information relating to the trade secrets of the claimant. The court found that the defendant had breached both his implied duty of fidelity and his fiduciary duty as director. The defence argued that the express clause only prevented 'disclosure' of business secrets and not the defendant's own use.

While the defendant succeeded on this argument, the court made a point of stating that there could be methods of use which would amount to making a disclosure if the way in which the secret knowledge was used made it quite clear to other people what the secret process or information was. Apart from such cases, however, the court did not feel that prohibiting disclosure does not prohibit use.

DEFENCES TO A BREACH OF CONFIDENCE ACTION

Public interest

The many ramifications of the public interest defence, for example in relation to the human rights aspects of freedom of speech and privacy, will not be dealt with in this section – only a fairly brief explanation will follow. The Human Rights Act 1998, s.12 and recent case law in this area will, however, be dealt with in Chapter 3 in relation to the obtaining of interim injunctions and freedom of expression.

In relation to any kind of confidential obligation or secret it is generally accepted that the overriding public interest is to make sure that the secret is kept. However, there may be instances where the public interest is better served by allowing confidences to be breached. A defence of public interest is therefore available in an action for breach of confidence – i.e., if it is in the public interest that the confidential information is made known to the public or to a government agency, e.g., for the prevention of crime (*Hellewell* v. *Chief Constable of Derbyshire* [1995] 1 WLR 804) or in the interests of public safety (*W* v. *Edgell* [1990] 1 Ch 359).

In *Lion Laboratories Ltd* v. *Evans & Others* [1984] 2 All ER 417, the defendants had been employed as technicians at the claimant company, which manufactured breathalysers used by the police to test drivers for alcohol, and had been involved in the development of the devices. The defendants became aware of information which cast doubt on the reliability of the breathalysers to give accurate results. The Court of Appeal, in balancing the public interest in maintaining the secrecy of the claimant's (undisputedly confidential) documents against the public interest in ascertaining the reliability of a testing device whose results could be used in criminal prosecutions, held in favour of the latter argument – the information was allowed to be published in the public interest.

The case of *Hubbard* v. *Vosper* [1972] 2 QB 84, involved the Church of Scientology and a former member of the Church. On joining the Church, the defendant agreed to keep certain information relating to the Church's activities secret. When the defendant left the Church, he published a book denouncing the Church's activities, which included information confidential to the Church. The Court of Appeal found that publication was justified as it was in the public interest, given what they saw as the dangerous nature of the Scientology cult.

The above cases therefore show that even where it would otherwise seem that there are clear obligations of confidence, in *Lion Laboratories* by virtue of their employment and in *Hubbard* by express agreement to keep certain matters secret, such obligations can be overridden if to do so is in the public interest.

The defence of morality

It should also be noted that the law of confidence cannot be called into play to protect material that is of a grossly 'immoral' nature, as in *Glyn* v. *Weston Feature Film Co Ltd* [1916] 1 Ch 261. As to what is considered immoral in contemporary society see *Stephens* v. *Avery* [1988] 1 Ch 457, which involved details of a lesbian relationship.

Third parties

In general a third party who receives information, knowing it to be confidential, or in circumstances where an obligation of confidence can readily be imposed, will be under an obligation of confidence. The cases of *Saltman* v. *Campbell* (p.18), *Fraser* v. *Thames Television Ltd* [1984] 1 QB 44, and *Argyll* v. *Argyll* [1967] Ch 303 illustrate that even though there may be no direct contractual link between the original discloser and the third-party recipient, the fact that the confidential nature of the information is clear to the recipient puts him under an obligation of confidence.

Confidential information may be also obtained completely innocently by accident, or may be obtained on purpose by dishonest means such as industrial espionage. In both of these situations there is no relationship at all between the parties, but the recipient of such information may still be bound by a duty of confidence.

It is obviously wrong to have a situation where the original, valid recipient of confidential information is held accountable under the law of confidence for disclosing information which was communicated to him by the confider, and an individual who dishonestly obtains what he knows to be confidential information is not to be held accountable. In the Australian case of *Franklin* v. *Giddings* [1978] Qd R 72, which involved the defendant stealing a cutting from one of the claimant's high-yielding nectarine trees in order to grow his own orchard, the court made an order for the destruction of the defendant's trees.

There is still however some uncertainty in the English law of confidence as to the precise level of protection afforded to confidential information gained outside a confidential relationship. In the case of *Malone* v. *Metropolitan Police Commissioner* [1979] 2 All ER 260, which involved telephone-tapping by the police, the court took a narrow approach, and did not grant an injunction preventing the prosecution using recordings made by the police as a result of authorised telephone-tapping.

In the later case of *Francome* v. *Mirror Group Newspapers* [1984] 2 All ER 408, which also involved telephone-tapping, but this time illegal tapping by an unknown person, a wider interpretation of the law was adopted and an injunction granted, based on breach of confidence, preventing publication of recordings. It therefore seems that in situations where there is no relationship between the parties, the court's view as to whether or not there is an obligation of confidence might be influenced by the way in which the information was acquired.

Now that we have established the nature of confidential obligations, the following chapter will look at the various courses of action available under English law to a party whose confidential information has been disclosed or is being threatened with disclosure.

CHAPTER 3

Remedies for breach of confidence

A wide range of remedies have been successfully applied in breach of confidence situations – injunctions, destruction and delivery-up, account of profits, constructive trusts and damages. Each of these will be dealt with in turn below, both generally and more specifically in relation to the law of confidence. As a claimant will normally wish to keep confidential information confidential, injunctions are in many cases the major remedy sought, and will receive the most attention in this chapter.

INJUNCTIONS

Being equitable, injunctions are discretionary, and the decision to grant an injunction will be influenced by factors such as the innocence of the defendant – for example, in the case of non-deliberate use of confidential information – and whether an injunction is really necessary or indeed effective.

In the context of confidential information, an injunction may serve two purposes. The first is to restrain the continued use of the information and the second is to restrain publication. The latter will not normally be appropriate where the information has already entered the public domain, subject to what has been said earlier in this book in relation to the springboard doctrine (see Chapter 2).

From the cases of *Coco* v. *Clark*, and *Seager* v. *Copydex*, it is clear that there are a number of factors which may be relevant when the court exercises its discretion as to whether to grant an injunction in cases involving confidentiality. A list of reasons which may make the grant of an injunction inappropriate might comprise:

(a)   subconscious or otherwise innocent copying by the defendant;
(b)   unwarranted or unjustified communication by the claimant;
(c)   the defendant using the information himself but pursuing an alternative in collaboration with another party;
(d)   the extent of the defendant's own contribution to a new successful product;

(e)   whether the information is of a personal or commercial nature;

(f)   whether the information taken is minor or otherwise mundane;

(g)   the fact that the information has become public; and

(h)   perhaps even the fact that the actual idea involved might be patentable – thereby requiring the claimant who wishes to have full title in the intellectual property to apply for a patent.

The main principles relating to the granting of injunctions are as applicable to matters involving confidential information as to any other subject matter, and the following paragraphs provide a general summary of the law in this area, with specific reference to breach of confidence where appropriate.

General principles relating to the grant of an injunction

As stated above, an injunction is an equitable remedy by which the court makes an order telling the defendant to do or not to do a specific act. Injunctions are widely available in cases concerning contract and tort, subject to certain requirements established by precedent.

Prohibitory and mandatory injunctions

Injunctions may be either prohibitory or mandatory. A prohibitory injunction restrains the defendant from doing something, and a mandatory injunction requires the defendant to take a positive step to carry out an action or to undo what he or she has done. It was described by Laddie J in *Psychometric Services Ltd* v. *Merant International Ltd* [2002] FSR 8 as 'obliging a party to do things for which he has no enthusiasm'.

The distinction between prohibitory and mandatory injunctions may be significant, because a claimant is supposed to couch a mandatory order in positive terms; but a mandatory order is generally harder to obtain than a prohibitory order. In relation to a breach of confidence action, the type of injunction sought will be a prohibitory one – stopping the defendant from disclosing confidential information. In practice, therefore, the almost invariable tendency is to phrase injunctions prohibitively wherever possible, e.g., an order restraining the defendant from allowing a state of affairs to continue.

In cases of breach of contract, a mandatory injunction to stop a breach is very rare, because in most cases it is to all intents and purposes an order of specific performance and will be sought as such. Given that there is no such thing as an interim specific performance, in the pre-trial stages of a claim an interim mandatory injunction may occasionally be sought.

Final and interim injunctions

A final injunction, sometimes known as a perpetual injunction (even if limited in time), is an order made at trial, or at the conclusion of an action if it does not get to trial, and orders in favour of one or both of the parties need making. However, most injunctions, and especially those in relation to breach of confidence, are sought as a matter of some urgency, and the claimant will not want to wait until trial as the damage will have been done by the time the case comes on for trial. The claimant will then seek an interim injunction, which will last only for a temporary period, until trial at the latest. Such an injunction, in cases of extreme urgency, may be sought without notice to the defendant, but if sought without notice will usually only be granted with permission to the defendant to apply to set it aside, or for a short time.

Given that interim injunctions cover a discrete period in time, the principles applicable to the grant of interim injunctions are quite different from the principles governing the grant of final injunctions.

Injunction for breach of contract

An injunction can only be granted in support of a legal or equitable right. If the claimant has no such right which needs protecting, or has no *locus standi* to bring the action to protect the legal rights of others, no injunction can be granted. Where there is a confidentiality agreement in place, it is the claimant's rights under that agreement which are being protected by the grant of an injunction. Given that the claimant needs to show a valid contract as well as an actual or threatened breach by the defendant, if the claimant can refer to a confidentiality agreement (detailing the specific areas of actual or threatened breach), that will obviously help the case.

Actual or threatened breach

Where the breach is actual, it will be relatively easy to prove. An injunction can readily be granted to restrain a continuing breach or to prevent the repetition of a breach. But sometimes the breach is merely threatened and lies in the future. In such circumstances a *quia timet* injunction (which is basically an injunction to prevent an action that has been threatened but has not yet violated the claimant's rights) may be granted to restrain the apprehended breach, but a high degree of proof is required. The claimant will have to prove a high probability of the breach occurring, and the likelihood of substantial damage resulting (*Attorney-General* v. *Manchester Corporation* [1893] 2 Ch 87; *Fletcher* v. *Bealey* (1885) 28 Ch D 688).

Prevention of breach of a negative stipulation

Confidentiality agreements usually contain clauses stipulating that the recipient of the information will not use the information for purposes other than a 'permitted purpose' and also not disclose the information to persons other than those specified in the agreement – both of which are negative stipulations.

As explained earlier, injunctions to restrain a breach of contract are usually prohibitory, and this is almost always the case in relation to breach of confidence actions. The need for an injunction arises where the defendant has done or threatens to do something he promised in the contract not to do: the injunction will therefore be in support of a negative stipulation in the contract. While such a stipulation will normally be express, it is worth noting that an injunction can also be granted to prevent a breach of an implied negative stipulation, provided that it does not amount to specific performance by the back door. An injunction will not, however, be granted in support of an *implied* negative stipulation in a contract of employment or personal service (*Mortimer* v. *Beckett* [1920] 1 Ch 571, though see *Lawrence David* v. *Ashton* [1991] All ER 385).

When is a final mandatory injunction appropriate?

The only circumstance in which a final mandatory injunction may be appropriate for breach of contract is where it is necessary to undo the effects of a breach by the defendant of a negative promise – a final mandatory injunction is therefore inappropriate where confidential information has already been disclosed by the defendant since the information cannot be 'undisclosed'. Final mandatory injunctions are appropriate in situations where the results or effects of an act of the defendant can be undone, for example the tearing down of a building built in contravention of a term to the contrary in a planning contract.

The terms of the injunction

Another advantage of ensuring that confidentiality obligations are set out in a confidentiality agreement relates to the fact that the terms of any injunction for breach of contract must be very carefully drawn. The claimant's rights are defined by the contract and so the claimant cannot get an order any wider in scope than that which the contract entitles him or her to – a well-drafted confidentiality agreement will include all necessary restrictions on use and disclosure.

The grant of an injunction

In general

Being an equitable remedy, an injunction will only be granted at the discretion of the court, and the usual equitable bars apply. A prohibitory injunction to restrain a breach of an express negative stipulation will normally be granted, and the grant of such an injunction will be aided if the claimant can indicate to the court a confidentiality agreement which clearly limits what the defendant can do with the confidential information.

Inadequacy of damages

The claimant must, of course, show that damages would not be an adequate remedy, but this is a much lower hurdle where the claimant seeks to prevent the defendant disclosing confidential information rather than where the claimant requires the defendant to do something. In the case of a prohibitory injunction to restrain a breach of contract, damages are not likely to be considered adequate (*Doherty* v. *Allman* (1878) 3 App Cas 709). However, damages may be adequate where the likely harm would be trivial, and a much stiffer test will be applied where the claimant seeks a mandatory injunction (*Shepherd Homes Ltd* v. *Sandham* [1971] Ch 340).

Other bars

Other bars that will prevent the grant of an injunction in a breach of confidence action include:

1. The fact that the contract is too vague: an order will not be made if it does not allow the defendant to understand precisely what he or she may or may not do. Of course this will not be an issue if there is a well-drafted confidentiality agreement in place.
2. Equity will not act in vain: an injunction will not be made if it will have no effect, for example if the information has already become public knowledge, as in one of the *Spycatcher* cases, where it was held that injunctions would not be granted against the *Observer* and *Guardian* newspapers preventing them from reporting on the contents of *Spycatcher* because publication abroad had effectively destroyed the secrecy of the book's contents.
3. Equity and clean hands: an injunction will not normally be granted to prevent a breach of contract by the defendant if the claimant is also in breach; and the claimant must show him or herself ready and willing to perform all his or her future obligations, e.g., in the case of a two-way confidentiality agreement, where both parties are disclosing information to each other.

4. Unreasonable delay: delay may lead to an injunction being refused, but this is by no means as serious a bar as it is to specific performance. Where, however, the claimant's delay effectively amounts to acquiescence in the defendant's breach, an injunction may not be granted (e.g., *Sayers* v. *Collyer* (1884) 28 Ch D 103). Unreasonable delay will amount to a bar in equity. This is known as the *doctrine of laches*, and again is in the court's discretion. How long a delay is unreasonable depends on the facts of the case, but in most circumstances not long is allowed.
5. Severe hardship: an injunction will be refused where it could cause severe hardship to the defendant. This is simply part of the court's overriding discretion to refuse an injunction where it would be unjust to grant it. However, in a case of hardship, the hardship must be severe, must not be brought about by the defendant's own acts, and must lead to injustice (see *Patel* v. *Ali* [1984] Ch 283).

Interim injunctions

Jurisdiction

Jurisdiction to grant interim injunctions in the High Court derives from the Supreme Court Act 1981 (SCA 1981), s.37. County court jurisdiction to grant interim injunctions derives from the County Courts Act 1984 (CCA 1984), s.38(1), which allows the court to make any order which could be made by the High Court if the proceedings were in the High Court.

The American Cyanamid *guidelines*

Although the granting of an injunction lies within the discretion of the court, the guidelines applicable to such applications are found in the leading case of *American Cyanamid* v. *Ethicon Ltd* [1975] AC 396. Generally the factors that the court will consider may be approached as a series of steps and the case for an injunction may fall at any point in the following sequence:

1. *Is there a serious question to be tried?* If the answer is yes (and it is often a fairly easy threshold to meet):
2. *Would damages be an adequate remedy?* That is, if the claimant succeeds at trial would he or she be adequately compensated by a (monetary) award – damages would be inadequate:
3. *If the defendant succeeded at trial,* i.e., he or she demonstrated a right to do the act(s) that the claimant sought to enjoin, *would the claimant's undertaking as to damages adequately compensate him or her?*
4. *Where does the balance of convenience lie?* The factors which the court will take into consideration and the weight attached to each will vary with each case but the question of whether damages would be an adequate remedy at the end of the trial is an important factor. This is particularly

apposite in confidential information cases where it is usually impossible to make publicly disclosed confidential information confidential again.

5. Where factors appear to be evenly balanced, the court will consider preserving the status quo. This means the state of affairs immediately before the issue of the writ, unless the claimant has delayed, in which case the status quo will be that existing immediately before the application.

In some established areas, including certain types of breach of confidence cases, the *American Cyanamid* approach is not strictly adhered to in determining whether to grant the injunction. Various factors, of which the ones gaining most prominence are those under the Human Rights Act 1998, may be of more or less importance depending on the nature of the dispute or third parties who may be affected by the granting of the injunction.

The *American Cyanamid* test of whether there is a 'serious issue to be tried' does not necessarily apply to applications for interim injunctions made to restrain media publications prior to trial (*Cream Holdings Ltd* v. *Banerjee* [2003] EWCA Civ 103). In *Cream Holdings*, a company was granted an interim injunction preventing a newspaper from publishing information about it obtained by a former employee. The newspaper and former employee appealed to the Court of Appeal against the order for the interim injunction on the grounds that the company had not satisfied the test in the Human Rights Act (HRA) 1998, s.12(3), relating to the circumstances in which the court can, in the light of the right to freedom of expression, restrain publication before trial.

Section 12(3) of the HRA 1998 prevents the court from restraining publication before trial unless it is satisfied that the appellant is likely to establish at trial that publication should not be allowed. The Court of Appeal held that the existence of this provision meant that it was not enough for the court simply to be satisfied, in accordance with the test in *American Cyanamid*, that there was a serious issue to be tried. Instead, s.12(3) required the court to put *American Cyanamid* firmly to one side and look at the merits and not just the balance of convenience. The appropriate test in such cases is therefore whether the applicant for an interim injunction has convincingly established a real prospect of success at trial.

Given that the availability of interim injunctions has been affected by the increasing impact of human rights considerations (see also *Naomi Campbell* v. *Mirror Group Newspapers Ltd* [2004] UKHL 22 referred to earlier, and *A* v. *B* [2002] 2 All ER 545, CA, which involved the rather colourfully tangled personal life of a Premier League footballer), the result is that in *some* situations the current position may be more restrictive than the standard *American Cyanamid* formula suggests. The *American Cyanamid* formula could be restated as below:

1. The claimant should have an arguable case except in breach of confidence cases where freedom of expression is at stake, in which case the

slightly higher standard of the claimant being likely to succeed at trial should apply;

2. The court should consider the balance of commercial convenience. If this is equal, the court should act to preserve the *status quo*. In breach of confidence cases where an issue of freedom of expression is at stake (as in *Naomi Campbell* v. *Mirror Group Newspapers Limited*, and *A* v. *B*) the court should weigh the claim of privacy as against that of the claim to freedom of expression and an injunction should only be granted where it is justified.

However, as stated above, the extent to which the *American Cyanamid* guidelines might not be strictly adhered to in a particular case depends upon careful consideration of all the issues. It therefore needs to be emphasised that whilst freedom of expression issues *may* crop up as a result of confidential information being disclosed between commercial entities (which is the main subject matter of this text) such issues may be treated in a different manner than outlined above.

Where obtaining an interim injunction would dispose of the action

It is important to distinguish between injunctions intended to be temporary in nature, i.e., effective until later trial, and those which would, in effect, dispose of the dispute because there are no further issues between the parties that need to be determined at a later trial. If this is the case, the *American Cyanamid* guidelines on the balance of convenience are not applied. Rather, it is appropriate for the court to consider the degree of likelihood that the claimant would have succeeded in establishing his or her right to an injunction at a trial on the merits. An injunction will only be granted if the claimant's case is overwhelming. See *Cayne* v. *Global Natural Resources plc* [1984] 1 All ER 225, CA.

Application procedure

Applications for interim injunctions are governed by the Civil Procedure Rules 1998, Parts 23 and 25. An application must be made by application notice supported by written evidence, usually in the form of a witness statement. This evidence should set out the facts on which the applicant relies. Under normal circumstances, the application notice should be served not less than three clear days before the hearing. However, in urgent cases, applications can be made without notice, even before the issue of a claim form. In these circumstances, an injunction can be made without the respondent being heard. However, the order made will only last until a return date, when there will be a further hearing.

DESTRUCTION OR DELIVERY-UP

Another equitable remedy, which might be available, depending upon the circumstances, is an order for the destruction of articles that have been made by using the confidential information, or which incorporate the tangible expression of such information. A successful claimant in a breach of confidence action is also entitled to the delivery-up to him of items which comprise the confidential information. A number of cases have dealt with the situation where an ex-employee has made a list of customers while employed by the claimant for use by him or by a subsequent rival employer, and such lists may be ordered to be delivered up (*Robb* v. *Green* [1895] 2 QB 315, per Lord Esher at p. 320). Similarly, books of formulae, drawings or specifications, or physical material may be ordered to be delivered up to the claimant. In the case of machinery that incorporates parts designed or made from information obtained in breach of confidence, a defendant may only have to deliver up those parts which actually constitute an infringement of the claimant's rights, and may thus dismantle the machine for that purpose.

Sometimes, a defendant may either undertake, or be ordered, to destroy infringing material (*Ackroyds* v. *Islington Plastics Ltd* [1962] RPC 97). Another option is that the material may be ordered to be delivered up for destruction by the claimant where any doubt is cast on the veracity of the defendant, in which case the court may deem it appropriate for the claimant to organise destruction of the material.

The usefulness of the order for destruction or delivery up was further demonstrated in the Australian case of *Franklin* v. *Giddings* [1978] Qd R 72, which involved illicit grafting of the claimant's nectarine buds by the defendant, and the court ordered for the destruction of the defendant's trees.

ACCOUNT OF PROFITS

An account of profits is another equitable remedy available for breach of contract (as was established by the decision of the House of Lords in *Attorney-General* v. *Blake* [2000] 4 All ER 385), where the court may order the defendant to account for all or some of the profits he or she has made through his or her breach of contract.

An account of profits is an alternative to damages, and, like other equitable remedies, is discretionary. An account of profits may be beneficial to the claimant if the information has actually been exploited commercially in breach of confidence. In *Peter Pan Manufacturing Corp* v. *Corsets Silhouette Ltd* [1963] 2 All ER 402 a manufacturer of brassieres made use of confidential information under a licence agreement. After the expiry of the licence agreement, the manufacturer continued to use the information, clearly in breach of confidence. In an action for breach of confidence, the claimant asked for an account of profits based on the whole of the profits accruing from the brassieres, but the defendant claimed that the account of profits should be based only on the profit resulting from the wrongful use of confidential information, that is, the profit relating to the parts of the brassieres incorporating the confidential information. The difference between the two sums was substantial and the claimant was awarded the higher sum because it was accepted by the court that the defendant would not have been able to make the brassieres at all without the use of the confidential information. However, in cases where only part of the profit concerned is attributable to the misuse concerned then the court will make an apportionment accordingly (*Hoechst Celanese International Corp* v. *BP Chemicals Ltd* [1999] RPC 203).

CONSTRUCTIVE TRUSTS

In breach-of-confidence cases, on the facts of a particular case, a constructive trust may arise in equity to provide an additional or alternative remedy. In general terms, a constructive trust can arise wherever there is a fiduciary relationship; it does not require the existence of a formal trust (*English* v. *Dedham Vale Properties Ltd* [1978] 1 WLR 93). The broad basis for finding a constructive trust is to prevent unjust enrichment (*Carl Zeiss Stiftung* v. *Herbert Smith & Co (No. 2)* [1969] 2 Ch 276; *James* v. *Williams* [2000] Ch 1, CA).

A constructive trust has been held to arise in the following circumstances:

(a) where a person in a fiduciary position gains any unauthorised personal benefit or profit from that position (see *Keech* v. *Sandford* (1726) Sel Cast King 61);

(b) where particular property is subject to a fiduciary duty (see *Tito* v. *Waddell* (*No. 2*) [1977] Ch 106);

(c) where property has been acquired as a result of information obtained by someone acting as a fiduciary (see *Boardman* v. *Phipps* [1967] 2 AC 46, but see *Sabnam Investments* v. *Dunlop Heywood* [1999] 3 All ER 652);

(d) where a stranger to a trust has actual or constructive knowledge of a trust and knowingly receives trust property; there are a very large number of reported cases dealing with the degree of knowledge required and whether there was sufficient proof of knowledge on the facts (see *Bank of Credit and Commerce International (Overseas) Ltd (in liquidation)* v. *Akindele* [2000] 4 All ER 221);

(e) a person who dishonestly procures or assists in breach of trust is liable to make good any resulting loss (see *Belmont Finance Corp Ltd* v. *Williams Furniture Ltd* [1979] Ch 250 and *Royal Brunei Airlines Sdn Bhd* v. *Tan* [1995] 3 WLR 64); and

(f) an agent acting for a trust can become a constructive trustee if he or she:

    (i) becomes chargeable with some part of the trust property; or

    (ii) knowingly assists in a dishonest or fraudulent design on the part of the trustee; or

    (iii) acts without proper instructions.

DAMAGES

Introduction

As stated earlier in this chapter, if information has been disclosed or used in some way in breach of confidence, then it will usually be too late for an injunction, but damages may be available. Damages may be calculated on the basis of conversion, breach of confidence being in the nature of an equitable tort. The fullest discussion of the relevant principles is to be found in *Seager* v. *Copydex Ltd (No. 2)* [1969] RPC 250, where it was said that the value of confidential information depends upon its nature, and one of the following two formulae would be appropriate:

1. If there *is nothing very special* about the information, and it could have been obtained by employing a competent consultant, then the value (for the purpose of damages) is the fee that consultant would charge.
2. If the information *is something special* involving an inventive step, then the value is the price a willing buyer would pay for it.

If the information in question is commercial in nature and used in the manufacture of an object which is sold or hired, then it would seem that damages should be assessed on the basis of the fee that the owner of the information reasonably might have expected if the information had been used with his licence.

Assessing damages for future infringement would be difficult using the second formula in *Seager* above. One might also question why a patent had not been applied for if there were an inventive step. A more appropriate approach would be that used in the *Coco* case, where an order was granted to the effect that the defendant should pay into a trust account a royalty on future products.

However, a market value approach is inappropriate where the claimant would not have thought of selling or licensing the confidential information to others. In the Canadian case of *Cadbury Schweppes Inc* v. *FBI Foods Ltd* [2000] FSR 491, the claimant acquired a company making a drink comprising tomato juice and clam broth, distributed under the name 'Clamato'. A former licensee made a new drink after termination of the licence, which was named 'Caesar Cocktail'. The claimant obtained a sample of this new drink, discovered the formula, and claimed that it had been made in breach of confidence. It was held that damages for the breach of confidence should be calculated on a 'but-for' basis as is usual with a tort. The claimant's lost opportunity was that the defendant had entered the marketplace some 12 months earlier than it would have otherwise done. However, the court would not unjustly enrich a confider by overcompensating for information considered 'nothing very special'.

In relation to innocent third parties, damages will be available, as a general rule, only if the third party knew or ought to have known that the information was subject to an obligation of confidence. Injunctions may be available, if appropriate, notwithstanding the innocence of the third party. Each case must be treated on its own merits and it is, effectively, a matter of satisfying the equity raised by the third party's intentions in relation to the information. Basic equitable principles should guide the courts in the exercise of their discretion in such matters and the interests of a third-party purchase without knowledge, actual or constructive, should, as is usually the case, be paramount.

Types of loss

Below is a thumbnail sketch of the three basic types of loss calculation, which are:

(a)   the expectation (or loss of bargain) basis;
(b)   the reliance (or wasted expenditure) basis; and
(c)   restitution.

The choice of which basis to use in calculating the claim for damages will depend on the kind of loss which has occurred as a result of the breach, and which method achieves the most advantageous result for the claimant.

The expectation (loss of bargain) basis

Damages for loss of bargain are forward-looking and are intended to put the claimant into the position he would have been in if the contract had actually been performed. This includes both the loss of the promised performance and the loss of profit resulting from not being able to put the performance to use.

All losses which are not too remote from the breach may be recovered, provided that the claimant has acted reasonably to mitigate his or her loss.

The reliance (or wasted expenditure) basis

Reliance loss arises where the claimant has expended money, which is then wasted in preparation for, or in partial performance of, the contract. It covers out-of-pocket expenses. Like the expectation/loss basis, the reliance/loss method aims to put the claimant in as good a position as he was in before the contract was made.

Reliance/loss will be claimed in cases where expectation loss is too speculative to recover (see e.g., *McRae* v. *Commonwealth Disposals Commission* (1950–51) 84 CLR 377; *Anglia Television* v. *Reed* [1972] 1 QB 60).

Restitution (unjust enrichment)

The third basis of calculating loss is where the claimant, in performing his obligations under the contract, has conferred a benefit on the defendant and wishes to claim back the benefit (or the value) given. For example, where the claimant has paid in advance for a product which is not delivered, he is entitled to the return of the money paid.

Choosing between expectation, reliance and restitution

Generally the claimant will be permitted to choose the method on which to base his or her claim, and the defendant is not entitled to insist that the claimant must pursue one basis over another. There are, however, several guiding principles which will apply. First, a claimant will not be permitted to claim damages for a reliance loss where this would compensate him, in effect, for a bad bargain, thereby putting him in a better position than he would have been in if the contract had been performed. Where the loss flows from having entered into the contract rather than from its breach, only the lower expectation/loss will be recoverable (see *CCC Films (London) Ltd* v. *Impact Quadrant Films Ltd* [1985] QB 16 and *C&P Haulage* v. *Middleton* [1983] 1 WLR 1461).

A claimant will not be permitted to claim for expectation/losses that are too speculative to be capable of satisfactory proof. In such a case, the claim will be limited to reliance losses and the value of a restitutionary claim.

A claim in restitution will only be permitted if the breach is a serious one which amounts to a total failure of consideration. If this is proved, restitution may be claimed even if the result is to leave the claimant in a better position than he would have been in if the contract had been performed.

CHAPTER 4

The employer–employee relationship

INTRODUCTION

As has been discussed earlier, an obligation of confidence may arise out of all manner of relationships, such as between a doctor and patient, a banker and his customer, and a solicitor and his client. In everyday commercial situations, however, the arena where one most often comes across confidentiality obligations is in the employment field, and the employer–employee relationship is therefore the subject of this chapter.

An employee owes a duty of confidence to his employer and this duty may be expressly stated in the contract of employment, and in any case will be implied by law. It can be said that an employee always has a duty to act in his employer's best interests together with a duty of good faith, and this will include a duty not to divulge confidential information about his employer's business to others without the consent of the employer. The sort of information concerned may be rather special, a 'trade secret' (e.g., a chemical formula), or it may be fairly ordinary, such as a customer list. As was discussed in Chapter 2, public interest exceptions may still apply, and the employee may be allowed to disclose the information in certain circumstances.

The obligation of confidence owed by an individual while in employment differs from that owed by a former employee to his old employer, and these two scenarios will where possible be dealt with separately. With regard to ex-employees, an important issue is that the ex-employee should be allowed to be able to earn a livelihood without unreasonable restriction. An area where the employer and the ex-employee sometimes disagree is whether the information in dispute should be regarded as a trade secret of the employer or as part of the general know-how of the employee's trade, which he should be allowed to take with him wherever he subsequently goes.

Some of the general principles of the law of confidence apply equally to employees as they do to other categories of person, but there are also some issues that are specific to employees, and which will be discussed in this chapter. These issues include:

1. The distinction that is made in employment law cases between 'trade secrets' and other types of confidential information.

2. The different levels of obligation of current employees and ex-employees.
3. Express obligations of confidentiality and implied obligations on employees under the general law.
4. Non-compete obligations on employees.

THE EXTENT OF THE DUTY OF CONFIDENCE IN EMPLOYMENT SITUATIONS

The duty owed by a current employee to his employer is generally fairly clear. If there is an employment contract in place then the duty of confidence arises from that contractual relationship (*Faccenda Chicken* v. *Fowler* [1985] 1 All ER 724), and in practice the confidentiality terms to be included in such a contract will generally be similar to those detailed in the precedents at the end of this book. In the absence of any express term, the duty of the employee to serve his employer with 'good faith and fidelity' will be implied into the employment contract (*Robb* v. *Green* [1895] 2 QB 315).

While a duty of fidelity will be implied in any event, the advantage of including express confidentiality terms in the employee's employment contract is that they will bring the issue of confidentiality obligations to the forefront of the employee's mind. Such express terms need to clearly state the exact remit of the material to be kept confidential. In situations where the information would probably be considered to be a trade secret by the employee, the employer does not have to specifically point this out (*Lancashire Fires Ltd* v. *SA Lyons Ltd* [1969] FSR 629), it is advisable for an employer to make clear to the employee the confidential nature of any material the employer reasonably feels needs to be protected.

As stated above, the duty of confidence during the course of employment is seen as a central aspect of the employee's general duty of good faith or fidelity. Another main aspect of this general duty of good faith and fidelity is the duty of an employee not to compete throughout the duration of the employment contract, which will normally include the duty of the employee not to compete in his spare time. The courts are more likely to identify a conflict if the employee knows of trade secrets that may be useful to a competitor and if he occupies a position with the employer where the expectation would be that he owes an exclusive duty to him. So, a lower-level employee, who works by the hour, will generally be less restricted from the point of view of how he uses his spare time than a member of the management team.

An employee may, in some cases, make preparations while he is employed in order to compete with his employer after he has left. Such preparations, however, generally may not include memorising a list of names of customers for later use.

As was the case in *Cranleigh Precision Engineering Ltd* v. *Bryant*, discussed earlier in Chapter 2, an employee may also have a positive duty to disclose information, which may be of benefit to his employer, which he encounters during his term of employment. In *Cranleigh*, the defendant was the managing director of the company, and therefore owed a fiduciary duty, which went beyond the general duty of good faith and fidelity to one's employer.

The main principles underlying breach-of-confidence cases involving employees were considered in *Faccenda Chicken* v. *Fowler* [1985] 1 All ER 724. The defendant was employed as a sales manager by the claimant company, whose business was selling fresh chickens. The defendant resigned from the claimant and set up a competing business covering the same client base, and also took eight of the claimant's former salespersons with him. During his employment, the defendant had acquired information concerning customers' names and addresses, routes, the quantity of goods usually ordered by customers, and the usual prices charged. The claimant's action was based on the assertion that the defendant had made improper use of the confidential information he had acquired during his employment. The employer's action for breach of confidence failed because the information was not of the type which an employee was bound, by an implied term in his contract of employment, not to use or disclose subsequent to the termination of employment – hence the importance of having express confidentiality terms in the employment contract to cover such a situation. Goulding J at first instance had classified employer–employee information into three categories:

(a) easily accessible information which was not confidential;

(b) confidential information which an employee could not use or disclose during his employment, but which, in the absence of an express covenant, he was at liberty to use subsequently; and

(c) trade secrets which he was not at liberty to disclose or use either during his employment or afterwards.

Goulding J placed the information carried away by the defendant in the second category. But since there was no express covenant, the defendant was held not to be liable. The claimant appealed. The Court of Appeal reached the same conclusion as the trial judge, but held that there was no second category of information which could be protected by an express restrictive covenant. The Court of Appeal stated that there were two categories of information: trade secrets which would be protected post-employment either by an express or implied contractual term and the rest, including information which may have had the necessary quality of confidence while the employee was employed, but ceased to do so once he had left. In this case, the information at issue did not amount to a trade secret, and so did not remain confidential post-employment.

Not surprisingly, problems often arise through the use or disclosure of confidential information by ex-employees, and, as referred to earlier, two competing interests need to be balanced: the employer's interest in keeping the information confidential, and the employee's need to be free to use his or her skill and knowledge to earn a living wherever he or she may choose. An employer will generally wish to limit the ability of an employee to compete using information acquired during the course of his employment. On the other hand, a former employee may wish to use this same information to further his own career prospects, even if this desire conflicts with the aims of his ex-employer.

In *Ocular Sciences Ltd* v. *Aspect Vision Care Ltd*, Laddie J stated that

> for public policy reasons, an employee is entitled to use and put at the disposal of new employers all his acquired skill and knowledge. . . . Where an employer's right to restrain misuse of his confidential information collides with the public policy, it is the latter which prevails.
> (*Ocular Sciences Ltd* v. *Aspect Vision Care Ltd* [1997] RPC 289 at p. 369)

However, in *Printers & Finishers Ltd* v. *Holloway* [1965] RPC 239, Cross J referred to information regarded as a separate part of the employee's store of knowledge which 'a man of ordinary honesty and intelligence would recognise to be the property of his old employer, and not his to do as he likes with' (at p. 255), and further added that the Court would restrain the use of such information via an injunction.

Indeed, what makes a potential employee attractive to potential employers is the knowledge and skill he has gained in his earlier jobs. It is not always easy, however, to separate such knowledge and skill from the previous employer's confidential information. The inclusion of express terms in an employee's employment contract restricting his use of confidential information after leaving his job is important, as the employer will not be protected to any great extent if there are no such terms included (*Printers & Finishers*). It is also useful to note, however, that even if there is an express term, the previous employer will still need to demonstrate that the information was over and above the employee's normal skill in his job and amounted to a trade secret.

WHAT IS GENERALLY MEANT BY 'TRADE SECRETS'?

Given that the term 'trade secrets' is referred to in much of the case law in this area, and whether or not information can be afforded protection will often depend on whether the relevant information can be classed as a trade secret, it is important to have an understanding of what is meant by the term.

In *Faccenda*, the Court of Appeal did not attempt to define trade secrets as such, but gave examples of trade secrets or their 'equivalent', including 'secret processes of manufacture such as chemical formulae' or 'designs and special methods of construction'. The meaning of the term was also widened to include 'other information which is of a sufficiently high degree of confidentiality to amount to a trade secret' including information about prices. The Court then identified four factors which are relevant to differentiating between trade secrets and other information, which would not be protected post-employment:

1. The nature of the employment. An employee who is accustomed to handling confidential information as part of his job may be expected to protect trade secrets better than one who is not.
2. The nature of the information. Is it the sort of information which meets the standard of a trade secret? In *Faccenda*, the example was offered of information which was given only to a limited number of employees.
3. Has the employer impressed upon the employee the confidentiality of the information? Stating that information is confidential does not necessarily make it so, but a warning that the information is confidential will assist the court in finding that it is.
4. Can the confidential information be easily isolated from other information which the employee acquired during his employment?

This last point above, the separability of the confidential information from other information, is quite important, as it can assist the court in coming to the conclusion that the information is actually confidential. This reasoning was followed in *AT Poeton (Gloucester Plating) Ltd* v. *Michael Ikem Horton* [2001] FSR 169, where the Court of Appeal found that the information that the claimant was asserting to be confidential did not have that status as it could not easily be isolated from other information which the employee was free to use, and Morritt LJ made the point that employers should use restrictive covenants in these situations, and if they did not then the Court would be reluctant to make a finding that such information fell into Goulding J's third category in *Faccenda*.

In *Faccenda*, the Court of Appeal found that the information about prices could not be isolated from the other information which was not protectable post-employment.

As one would expect, the duty of good faith and fidelity owed by a former employee is not as great as the duty owed by an employee during his employment. As discussed above, during employment, there is an implied term in the contract of employment that the use or disclosure of confidential information, even though it may not amount to a trade secret, will be a breach of the duty of good faith. By contrast, post-employment, the implied term will cover the obligation not to use or disclose trade secrets, but it will not cover all the information acquired by an employee during the course of his employment.

In *Printers & Finishers*, Cross J gave as an example of this sort of information the printing instructions which were given to the defendant by the claimant. During his employment, it would have been a breach of confidence for the defendant to disclose these instructions to a third party. But, according to Cross J, many of these instructions were not really 'trade secrets'. While the defendant was clearly not entitled to take a copy of the instructions away with him, 'in so far as he carried them in his head', he was entitled to use them for his own benefit or for the benefit of a future employer. In effect, upon leaving his employment, they had become part of his general knowledge or know-how.

Being able to separate out different types of information is indeed vital in carrying out the exercise of distinguishing between the know-how and general knowledge which the employee is able to take away from his employment and confidential information which he cannot take away, which is discussed below.

CONFIDENTIAL INFORMATION OR KNOW-HOW?

In a more recent Court of Appeal decision on employee secrets, *FSS Travel and Leisure Systems* v. *Johnson* [1999] FSR 505, Mummery LJ cited with approval the distinction drawn by Cross J in *Printers & Finishers* between trade secrets which are owned by the employer and the general skill and knowledge which an employee is entitled to take with him.

In *Printers & Finishers*, the defendant was a manager of the claimants' printing factory. While still in their employment, he contacted another company about setting up a competing printing plant. In addition, he showed employees of the other company around the claimant's factory, showed them samples of the claimant's products and ordered a machine of the claimant's design for the use of the other company. The claimant sought to restrain the defendant from misusing its confidential information. According to Cross J (at p. 255), if the contested information could 'fairly be regarded as a separate part of the employee's stock of knowledge which a man of ordinary honesty and intelligence would recognise to be the property of his old employer and not his own to do as he likes with' then the information would be protected as confidential.

On the other hand, general knowledge of the claimant's plant and process, of the difficulties encountered in production, and ways round them (which the employee has discovered for himself by trial and error during the employment) were not trade secrets. In this case, according to Cross J, the defendant's skill in manipulating a printing plant which he had acquired during his employment could not be separated from 'his general knowledge of the . . . printing process' and Cross J did not think that a man of average intelligence and honesty would consider there was anything improper in his putting his memory of particular features of his late employers' plant at the disposal of his new employer.

In *FSS Travel*, the defendant was employed as a computer programmer at the claimant company. There was a non-compete clause in the defendant's contract stipulating that for a period of one year after leaving the claimant's employment, he would not engage in any competing business. The defendant left and took up employment with a competitor. The claimant sought to enforce the post-termination covenants. At first instance, it was held *inter alia* that the claimant had trade secrets to protect but that the scope of the restrictive covenant was unreasonable. The claimant appealed. The Court of Appeal dismissed the appeal but on the grounds that there was no confidential information capable of being protected. According to Mummery LJ, the determination of whether the employee's knowledge constitutes confidential information or know-how is a question of fact, to be decided by examining all the evidence, considering not only the factors which had been identified in *Faccenda* but also the extent to which the information is in the public domain and the likely damage to the employer if the information is disclosed. During his employment, the defendant had acquired skill, experience, know-how and general knowledge relating to the computer systems rather than a separate identifiable body of objective trade secrets to which the claimant was entitled. The express covenant was therefore invalid and the employer had no trade secrets legitimately protectable by the imposition of a covenant.

RESTRICTIVE COVENANTS AND THE EX-EMPLOYEE

Post-termination non-compete and confidentiality provisions should not be drafted too widely. Terms that are too wide may be held unenforceable as being in restraint of trade, and the courts will not uphold a restrictive covenant whose sole aim is to protect an employer from competition per se, rather than to protect some specific subject matter for which the employer can legitimately claim protection, such as trade secrets (*Stenhouse Australia Ltd* v. *Phillips* [1974] AC 391, PC). The burden of proof is usually on the employer to show that any such covenant is reasonable.

It follows, according to Neil LJ in *Faccenda*, that a trade secret can be protected post-employment by an express term in a restrictive covenant. However, the second category of information identified by Goulding J, which is less than a trade secret, cannot. To allow such protection would unreasonably expand the scope of the subject matter of restrictive covenants and inhibit competition. In effect, according to the Court of Appeal in *Faccenda*, Goulding J's second category of information becomes, post-employment, an aspect of the know-how and general knowledge which is acquired by the employee as part of his job and which cannot be subject to restraint.

Non-compete and confidentiality terms, or covenants in restraint of trade, have the general aim of stopping the employee from working for a competitor or setting up his own competing business within a specified geographical area and for a specified period of time. The courts will not enforce a covenant it sees as too wide in terms of area or time, and will consider the effect of both aspects in tandem, as in *Herbert Morris Ltd* v. *Saxelby* [1916] 1 AC 688, where a restriction that an engineer could not work for a competitor anywhere as an engineer for seven years was held to be unenforceable. However, in *Fitch* v. *Dewes* [1921] AC 158, where a solicitor's clerk was prohibited from entering into the employment of another solicitor within a seven-mile radius of Tamworth Town Hall, even though the restriction was indefinite in terms of time the clause was held to be valid because the geographical area covered was small.

The manner in which many businesses operate today was taken into account in *Office Angels Ltd* v. *Rainer-Thomas* [1991] IRLR 214, where it was held that since the employer's business was carried out by taking orders over the telephone, a geographical area restriction was inappropriate and too wide.

Many covenants in restraint of trade, as well as comprising non-compete clauses, will also often include non-solicitation clauses, and again, such clauses should not be drafted too widely, see *Austin Knight (UK) Ltd* v. *Hinds* [1994] FSR 52. The importance of the employer acting reasonably when drafting non-compete and non-solicitation clauses cannot be overstated. If a covenant in restraint of trade is held by the court to be too wide, it will be void. Moreover, the court will not reduce the remit of the clause and apply a less wide clause instead, and the employer, by including such an unreasonable clause, will then have lost all possible protection it could have had under the clause (*JS Mont (UK) Ltd* v. *Mills, The Independent*, 7 January 1993).

DRAFTING IMPLICATIONS

From the above discussion, it can be seen that it is possible to improve the employer's position under general law, to some extent, by drafting appropriate confidentiality and non-compete terms as part of the contract of employment. However, if the employer goes too far, the obligations may become unenforceable. Points to bear in mind include the following:

1. In the 'grey area' between trade secrets and general skill and knowledge, an employer may wish to categorise certain information (e.g., in the contract of employment) as being in the former, rather than the latter category. Any such categorisation should be as specific as possible. It is not easy to predict whether the court will agree with any such categorisation, but it may be 'worth a try'.
2. Generally, the draftsperson should bear in mind the need to demonstrate to the court that any obligations and restrictions are reasonable, particularly (but not only) with respect to post-termination obligations and restrictions.

OBLIGATIONS OF THE EMPLOYER: THE DATA PROTECTION ACT

It is often forgotten that, in employee–employer situations, the employer will generally also owe a duty of confidence to his employee. The employer's personnel records will often include all manner of personal information in relation to their employees, which should generally not be divulged without the employee's permission. The Data Protection Act 1998 applies when one is dealing with information of a personal nature, and most employers are required to register with the Information Commissioner, detailing the exact types of information they process and the purpose of the processing that the business carries out in its capacity as a 'Data Controller' under the Act. Further details of the requirements under the Data Protection Act can be obtained from the Information Commissioner's website at www.informationcommissioner.gov.uk.

Practice

CHAPTER 5

Commercial strategy

ADVISING THE CLIENT: PRELIMINARY QUESTIONS

Sometimes, a client will send a draft confidentiality agreement (CDA) to his solicitor with the simple question: is this OK to sign? Even where the solicitor is familiar with his client's business activities in general, it is important to ask some basic questions before advising, such as those set out below.

1. *Who is disclosing information*: the client or the other party or both?
2. *What type of information is to be disclosed?* For example, is it to be commercial information such as business proposals or financial accounts, or scientific information such as the results of experiments or an unpublished patent application, or some other category of information, such as information gleaned at a celebrity's wedding that is to be the subject of an exclusive article in a glossy magazine?
3. *How sensitive is the information?* Some types of information are more confidential than others: for example, the formula for Coca-Cola (which apparently has been a trade secret for more than a century) may be more valuable as a secret than, say, some unpublished accounts that will be filed with Companies House within the next few months.
4. *Upside:* why is the information to be disclosed and what advantages are there in disclosing? Often, the answer is that the information will enable the recipient of the information to progress a project of some kind, e.g., to consider whether to enter into a further agreement with the disclosing party, or to provide a service to the disclosing party.
5. *Downside:* what adverse consequences will follow if the information becomes publicly known? Will this result in the loss of a competitive advantage, or the opportunity to file patents, or some other adverse consequence?
6. *Upside versus downside:* how do the advantages or potential of disclosure of the information compare with the disadvantages that may result from disclosure of the information, e.g., if it is misused by the recipient or is leaked into the public domain?
7. *What is the 'shelf-life' of the confidential information?* will it become publicly known after a year or two, or will it remain as a valuable secret for a much longer period?

Once the adviser has the answers to these and other questions, the adviser can give some useful advice, depending on the client's circumstances.

WHERE THE CLIENT IS TO DISCLOSE INFORMATION

Should the information be disclosed at all?

Clients sometimes have a misguided faith that CDAs provide a near-watertight guarantee that their information will be protected. They may need to be warned of the limitations of CDAs, including the following.

Injunctions

The main remedy for breach of a CDA is an injunction to prevent the recipient from disclosing or using the information further. But the owner of the information may not be aware that any breach is about to take place, and once the information has been disclosed, it may be too late (see below). Moreover, applying for an interim injunction in a breach of confidence action can be an expensive business: specialist firms of intellectual property solicitors often quote figures in the region of £50,000 or more for bringing such an action in the High Court.

Damages

Prevention is better than cure; once information has entered the public domain it may be impossible to make it confidential again, and the most that may be available is a claim for damages against the party that disclosed it. Damages may not be an adequate remedy: often, confidential information has a potential value rather than a realised value. For example, a new process for making a drug may be an extremely valuable piece of information once the drug is put on the market, but that may be several years after the information is discovered. At the time of discovery, the information only has a potential value. Any award of damages is unlikely to compensate the 'owner' of the information fully for his potential lost profits from the sale of a drug that may never reach the market.

Proving breach

It is not always easy to prove that the recipient has breached the CDA. Some of the leading, reported cases concern situations where wrongdoing is easy to establish, as in the case of a frozen chicken salesman who was caught with his former employer's confidential customer-lists in his possession (see the *Faccenda* case, referred to at p. 36). But not all cases are so clear-cut. Take the example of where the confidential information concerns a manufacturing process. The recipient does not imitate that process exactly in his own factory, but uses the information that he has learned to develop an improved process. Or, the recipient may have several alternative processes under consideration, and the information that he obtains from the disclosing party may cause the recipient to stop working on one of his processes and develop a different one. It may be very difficult to prove that his choice of a new process is derived from, or has benefited from knowledge of, the disclosing party's process. But the disclosing party may suffer loss from the breach, because he has given a competitive advantage to the recipient for which he is not compensated.

Despite these limitations on the value of a CDA, the client may take the view that the commercial benefits of disclosing the information under a CDA (e.g., interesting the recipient in entering into a further agreement) outweigh the risks associated with disclosure. If so, then some further issues may need to be addressed, including the following.

Which information should be disclosed?

Sometimes, it may be commercially desirable to provide some confidential information to the recipient, but to withhold the 'crown jewels', i.e., the most sensitive and confidential parts of the information. Or, it may be prudent to disclose the most sensitive information at a later date, e.g., when a further agreement has been reached, or when a patent application has been filed.

Should any of the information be subject to special security precautions?

Where particularly sensitive information is to be disclosed, additional security precautions may be thought useful, including those set out below.

1. Disclosing the information to a trusted intermediary, with strict instructions as to what the intermediary may do with the information. For example, the intermediary might confirm to the recipient that the information includes some vital element, without disclosing the details of that vital element.
2. Disclosing the information to a named individual within the recipient's organisation, and entering into an additional CDA with that individual, specifying what he may do with the information (e.g., he may not disclose the information to anyone else within the organisation, but may advise his colleagues whether certain information has been disclosed to him and whether it appears to be robust or complete information on the subject under discussion). This is a variation on the previous paragraph.
3. Providing copies of the (written or otherwise recorded) information that are each individually numbered, so that the source of any copies

made can be traced, and at the same time prohibiting the making of copies.

4.   Where information is provided electronically, consider providing it in a format that cannot be amended, e.g., to delete any confidentiality or ownership statements or create modified versions of the information.[1]

5.   Providing access to the information under controlled conditions, and not allowing copies of the information to be made. For example, in corporate transactions, information about the company being sold is sometimes made available in a 'data room' at the selling party's solicitors.

6.   Including particularly 'tough' provisions in the CDA – this subject is considered further below, in the discussion of the terms of CDAs.

Maintaining records and other administrative procedures

As well as signing a suitably worded CDA, it may help the disclosing party to protect his interests in his confidential information if some practical procedures are adopted, including those set out below.

1.   Ensure that all information that is disclosed is prominently marked as 'confidential'. Where documents are generated electronically, this can conveniently be done by adding a header or footer to the document. Alternatively a rubber stamp should be used. (See further p. 102 for an example of a confidentiality statement that might be included in documents.)

2.   Where information is disclosed orally, make a note of what has been disclosed, and consider sending this note to the other party and/or try to get the other party to agree the note. This may be useful irrespective of whether the agreement requires orally disclosed information to be confirmed in writing. (For a discussion of whether such a provision should be included in the CDA, see further p. 63.)

3.   Generally, maintain records of exactly what information has been disclosed. This is of practical importance and will also provide evidence in case litigation over the CDA is required.

4.   Channel all disclosures through a nominated individual within the disclosing party's organisation. This may reduce the risk of inadvertent disclosure of other information that is not meant to be disclosed.

5.   Monitor the recipient's use of the confidential information, e.g., by holding regular meetings throughout the term of the CDA to discuss what use is being made of it, and to ask for copies of any reports or

---

[1] This probably means something more secure than a 'read-only' format in a word-processed document. It is understood that some PDF (e.g., Adobe Acrobat) formats may have the facility of a more secure read-only format that is more difficult to override. Such a measure may be of limited value, particularly where documents can be printed out then scanned into the computer again and converted into word-processed documents.

results that the recipient has generated using the confidential information. In suitable cases, it may be desirable to maintain a watching brief (or instruct others to do so) over any new products or other developments that are announced by the recipient, as well as any patent applications that it may file, with a view to establishing whether these developments may have made use of the disclosing party's confidential information.

6.   Maintain a diary system to ensure that at the end of any agreed period of disclosure, the information is retrieved from the recipient.

WHERE THE CLIENT IS TO RECEIVE INFORMATION

As a recipient of confidential information, one's client may have (some) different priorities to when he is disclosing confidential information.

Record-keeping

Assuming that he intends to abide by the terms of the CDA, the recipient may be just as concerned as the disclosing party to maintain proper records of what has been disclosed to him, e.g., so as to avoid exaggerated claims from the disclosing party in the event of a dispute.

Which information should be received?

The recipient may wish to limit any disclosure to a particular category of information. For example, the recipient may require that the CDA include a definition of the subject matter that is to be covered by the CDA. By implication, all information outside this definition would not be subject to the terms of the CDA.

Possible reasons why the recipient might wish to include such a definition include those set out below.

1.   Simply as an administrative matter, so that the parties know the general subject matter of their discussions and can involve appropriate people in the discussions.
2.   So as to avoid receiving information in an area where the recipient has generated its own information and does not wish its development team to be 'contaminated' with the disclosing party's information. The recipient might wish to avoid arguments that the disclosing party has an interest in any subsequent development or use of the recipient's information. For example, the disclosing party might argue that he first provided some of the information that the recipient subsequently developed or, less directly, that the recipient would not have developed his own

information if he had not received further valuable information (e.g., corroboration that it worked or was considered useful) from the disclosing party.

As a variant on the above, the CDA might expressly state that if certain types of information are disclosed, the recipient will not be bound by any obligations of confidentiality with respect to such information. The author of this book has seen documents entitled 'non-disclosure agreement' which are, in effect, an acknowledgement (or even a warranty) by the disclosing party that it will not disclose any confidential information to the recipient and, if it does so, the recipient will not have any confidentiality obligations to the disclosing party with respect to that information.

To whom should the information be disclosed?

Sometimes, the recipient will wish to channel any receipt of information through one or more named representatives of the recipient party. There are a number of possible reasons for this, including those set out below.

1. The subject matter of the confidential information may be confidential and may only be known to a few people within the recipient organisation. An example of this might be early-stage discussions over a possible merger between the disclosing party and the recipient. The recipient may wish to provide in the CDA that all communications between the parties must be between named individuals.

2. As an administrative matter, the recipient may wish to ensure that all information is channelled through named individuals, so that the recipient may be sure what information has been disclosed and is subject to the CDA, and to whom that information should most appropriately be forwarded.

3. The recipient may wish a named individual to act as a filter to prevent the recipient organisation from inadvertently receiving information in an area in which it has generated its own information. The perceived risk may be that the recipient's scientists or other information-generators would be 'contaminated' by learning third-party information that they cannot unlearn, thereby enabling the disclosing party to argue that it has an interest in any subsequent commercial developments that the recipient may make in that field. Where companies use this kind of filtering mechanism, they sometimes require any information to be disclosed first to a non-specialist (e.g., someone in the Company Secretarial department), who knows enough about the subject to recognise potentially 'dangerous' information, but who is not part of the team that develops the in-house information.

Other security measures

The recipient may wish to provide in the CDA that all orally disclosed information be identified as confidential at the time of (oral) disclosure and confirmed in writing that is marked confidential and sent to the recipient within, say, 30 days of the oral disclosure. The terms of CDAs are discussed generally in Chapter 6.

WHERE BOTH PARTIES ARE TO DISCLOSE AND RECEIVE INFORMATION

Two-way CDAs tend to be fairly evenly balanced in their terms, as each party is both a discloser and a recipient of confidential information. The policy issues that arise are the same as those already discussed above.

OTHER 'POLICY' ISSUES

With some types of organisation it may be queried whether they should enter into CDAs at all and, if they do, whether they are fully capable of complying with the CDA's terms.

The most obvious example that comes to mind is universities. One of the main purposes of a university is to disseminate knowledge. The free exchange of information and ideas between academics is an important part of what they do for a living. Confidentiality obligations do not sit easily with the academic mindset. Where research is classified as 'academic research', it may be incompatible with that status for it to be kept permanently secret.

Another aspect of academic life is that academics are not always inclined to obey the instructions of their employers, particularly those issued by the administrative functions such as research contracts and technology transfer departments. Even where they are willing in principle to comply, they may not always have implemented the necessary procedures to protect the confidential information against inadvertent disclosure or leakage. These are of course generalisations: some academics are very careful and diligent about protecting confidential information.

For these reasons, arguably, universities ought to be cautious about accepting confidentiality obligations. (On the other side of the coin, they should perhaps be cautious about granting rights in confidential information, as in the case of know-how licences.)

Other organisations that may be ill-equipped to comply with the obligations of CDAs include some charities, and some subsidiary companies. Some smaller charities may not have the management structure or procedures to ensure compliance with the terms of CDAs, and in this respect may be similar to universities.

Where a subsidiary company enters into a CDA on behalf of all of its affiliates, including its parent company, it may be queried whether it has the power to bind its parent company. This is discussed further in the section on the detailed terms of CDAs, below.

Some organisations refuse to enter into CDAs at all, or in some circumstances. For example, it can sometimes be difficult for a company to persuade its financial brokers and sponsors to enter into tightly worded CDAs.

IS A CDA NECESSARY?

In some relationships, confidentiality obligations are implicit and do not need to be reduced to a written CDA. The most obvious example for readers of this book may be a solicitor's obligation of confidentiality to his client. In the author's experience, clients occasionally suggest that their solicitors enter into a CDA but the client can usually be persuaded that this is not necessary because of the very strict obligations that arise under the Law Society's Code of Conduct.

Increasingly, CDAs seem to be referring to a party's rights to disclose information to its professional advisers. Previously, this was probably thought to be unnecessary, at least in the case of solicitors.

As has previously been mentioned, confidentiality obligations may arise in the absence of a CDA, and in the absence of a special relationship such as solicitor and client, because of the circumstances in which the information was disclosed. However, as has also been mentioned, parties would generally be well advised to specify their obligations in a contract rather than rely on the general law of confidence.

CHAPTER 6

Drafting and negotiation

WHO SHOULD DRAFT THE CDA?

In the author's experience, there is no convention concerning which party should draft the CDA: they are sometimes prepared by the disclosing party, and sometimes by the recipient.

Some organisations, when presented with a CDA to sign, respond by proposing their own favoured form of CDA. The argument that is sometimes put forward, is that this is their company's policy. A less aggressive stance, sometimes encountered, is that using their own form of CDA will avoid the need for them to obtain legal advice on the externally drafted CDA. Particularly in large organisations, it is the easy option to propose one's own standard CDA. But a little 'push-back' will sometimes be enough to get the organisation to consider the externally drafted CDA.

Ultimately, what matters is the substance of the document rather than its provenance. Sometimes, the parties' CDAs will look very different from one another, particularly if one or both parties propose a one-sided document. It can sometimes smooth the negotiation of the CDA if it is prepared as a two-way CDA, even if one of the parties is not expected to contribute much in the way of confidential information.

HOW DETAILED SHOULD THE CDA BE?

The more important and valuable the information, the more concerned one would usually be to cover all confidentiality issues thoroughly. Although the core issues that are usually addressed in CDAs are similar, the length of an individual CDA can vary between one page and, say, ten pages of text. Most tend to be two or three pages long, and for the disclosure of routine, albeit confidential information, this level of detail will generally be considered sufficient. Examples of brief, and more detailed, CDAs appear later in this book (see p. 91 onwards).

FORMAT OF THE CDA

Simple CDAs are often drafted in the form of a letter from one party to the other, which the recipient of the letter signs and returns to indicate his agreement to comply with its terms. Whether a CDA is drafted in this format or in a conventional 'agreement' format, or in some other format, is a matter of stylistic preference. English law does not generally prescribe a particular format for commercial agreements made 'under hand'; indeed such contracts do not generally need to be in writing in order to be legally binding. As a practical matter, CDAs should be in writing, if only to provide evidence of the terms that have been agreed.

Where the CDA is to be executed as a deed, the formalities for deeds must be complied with.[1] It is assumed that readers are familiar with the requirements of English law for a contract to be legally binding and for a contract to be executed as a deed rather than as a contract 'under hand'.[2] One of the main reasons why parties might wish to execute their CDA as a deed is concern as to whether consideration has been given for the confidentiality undertakings. Consideration is not required in order for an undertaking given in a deed to be legally binding. If the parties do not wish to execute their CDA as a deed, an alternative way of dealing with this issue is to include in the CDA an obligation to pay a nominal amount of consideration, e.g., £1. In practice, consideration will often be found from the circumstances of the disclosure of the information. Or it may be possible to argue that the CDA is binding under the equitable law of confidence (as to which, see Chapter 1). Nevertheless, the issue of consideration should not be overlooked.

Another reason is that the limitation period for bringing an action for breach of contract is six years in the case of a contract under hand, and twelve years in the case of a contract executed as a deed.

The terms of the CDA will now be reviewed, clause by clause.

PARTIES TO THE CDA

The main types of parties to CDAs tend to be:

- individuals;
- UK companies;

---

[1] For a discussion of the formalities for agreements 'under hand' and agreements executed as deeds, respectively, and a summary of the main categories of agreement that must be in writing or executed as deeds, see Anderson M., *Drafting and Negotiating Commercial Contracts*, Butterworth, 1997.

[2] In particular, intention to create legal relations, the capacity of the parties, offer and acceptance, consideration, certainty of terms, complete agreement and legality of subject matter.

- non-UK companies; and
- other organisations, e.g., a university incorporated in the UK by Royal Charter.

Where information is to be disclosed to an individual who works for an organisation, it will usually be the organisation that executes the CDA rather than the individual. Sometimes, it may be appropriate to have both of them sign the CDA. For example, if the recipient is an academic scientist working for a university, it is not uncommon to ask both the scientist and the university to sign the CDA. In this example, academic scientists are sometimes perceived as being less closely aligned with the interests of their employer (i.e., the university) than would be the case with a scientist employed by a commercial company. Therefore, it may be appropriate to have the individual sign the CDA as well as the university.

Where a CDA is signed on behalf of a university, the other party to the CDA may wish to check that it has been signed by a representative of the central administration of the university and not just by the individual scientist or his head of department, neither of whom may be, in fact, authorised to sign agreements on behalf of the university.

Where an individual signs a CDA, his or her home address, rather than work address, should usually be stated in the CDA.

Where a company enters into a CDA, it is important to ensure that the full, correct company name is used, including any words or abbreviations such as 'Limited' or 'Inc'. The country of incorporation should generally be stated, particularly in relation to overseas companies. In the case of US companies, the state of incorporation should also be stated.

Where contracts are made between parties based in different jurisdictions, they sometimes each agree to appoint an 'agent for service' within the other party's jurisdiction. This enables the other party to serve a writ on the first party within the other party's jurisdiction. It should be said that this type of arrangement is hardly ever encountered in simple CDAs. One reason for this may be that the most common type of action for breach of a CDA is an urgent application for an interim injunction, and these are usually best applied for in the defendant's home territory.

STATUS, CAPACITY AND RELATIONSHIP OF THE CONTRACTING PARTIES

Affiliates

Sometimes, CDAs include a reference to the affiliates of each of the contracting parties. Where such references are included, affiliates are usually defined in the CDA as including subsidiaries and parent companies of the contracting party, as well as any fellow subsidiaries of the same parent company. The CDA will then usually provide for one or more of the following:

    (a)   permit disclosure of confidential information to an affiliate of the party that receives the information under the CDA and/or employees and directors of such affiliates;

    (b)   extend the receiving party's obligations so as to bind, additionally, affiliates of the receiving party;

    (c)   extend the receiving party's obligations so as to cover information provided by an affiliate of the disclosing party.

Where such provisions are included, it is not always made clear whether the affiliates are intended to be a party to the CDA. Under English law, contractual *obligations* cannot generally be imposed upon a legal entity that is not a party to the contract; this principle is known as 'privity of contract'. Following a change in the law, *rights* under contracts can be extended to third parties who are not parties to the contract (under the Contracts (Rights of Third Parties) Act 1999).

Thus, where a CDA allows the receiving party to disclose information to its affiliates, the CDA should also make clear whether and how the affiliates are to be bound by the receiving party's obligations under the CDA. This can generally be done in one or more of the following ways.

1.   State in the CDA that the receiving party signs the CDA on its own behalf and on behalf of, and as agent for, each of its affiliates. There is a practical issue as to whether the receiving party actually has such authority to sign on behalf of affiliates. Although the disclosing party will have a remedy against the receiving party if it turns out that it did not have such authority, disclosing parties are usually more concerned to prevent their confidential information being misused or made public, than to have a right of damages.

2.   State in the CDA that the receiving party may only pass on the disclosing party's information to affiliates who have undertaken to comply with the receiving party's obligations under the CDA. This is probably less satisfactory for the disclosing party than the first alternative, above.

3.   Add the affiliates as additional parties to the CDA and have each of them sign the CDA. This may present practical difficulties, particularly if the receiving party is part of a large group of companies.

Where information is provided to the receiving party by an affiliate of the disclosing party, it may be desirable to clarify whether such information is covered by the terms of the CDA and whether the affiliate is to have any right to sue the receiving party if it breaches the terms of the CDA.

Subsidiaries

As a practical matter, it may be thought undesirable to enter into a CDA with (only) a subsidiary company within a group of companies, unless:

(a)   it is clear that the information will be kept within that subsidiary and not disclosed to other companies, or the employees of other companies, within the group; or

(b)   the subsidiary provides convincing evidence that it is in a position to control the compliance by its parent and associated companies with the subsidiary's obligations under the CDA.

In such circumstances, as a minimum, it may be necessary to have the ultimate parent company sign the CDA, instead of or as well as the subsidiary in question. Although there is no guarantee that a parent company is in a position to control the behaviour of its subsidiaries, this may be more likely to be the case than that the subsidiary can control the behaviour of its parent(s). Where the parent alone signs the CDA, it may be desirable to include a warranty that it is able to and will ensure that its affiliates comply with the provisions of the CDA, and to make it a condition of disclosure to the affiliate that the affiliate has agreed to be bound by its terms.

These are pragmatic solutions and do not provide as good a legal protection as having each disclosee enter into a CDA directly with the disclosing party.

Agents and brokers

Sometimes, CDAs are executed by parties who are acting as agents for another party. For example, where the subject matter of the confidential discussions is a proposed corporate merger or acquisition, some discussions may be initiated by, or conducted through, a party's broker or shareholder representative. In such situations, it may be appropriate for the other party to the CDA to seek to verify the agent's authority to act as agent and/or to require the principal to sign the CDA as well as the agent.

Alternatively, a party may wish to clarify that the other party is not acting as an agent or broker, and to this end might include wording such as the following in the CDA:

> ABC is acting in relation to the possible Investment as principal and not as agent or broker for or in concert with any other person.

Other related parties

Sometimes, CDAs are drafted so that they apply to information that is disclosed not only to the receiving party, but also to any related parties of the receiving party, as in the following definition:

> the Recipient or its affiliates and/or its and their directors, officers, employees, agents, advisers, attorneys, accountants, consultants, bankers, financial advisers and other representatives (the 'Related Parties')

Direct and indirect disclosures

Sometimes, CDAs define confidential information as including information that is disclosed to the receiving party 'directly or indirectly' by the disclosing party. Such a phrase is usually included to deal with the situation where the information originated from the disclosing party and was obtained by the receiving party, but the latter did not obtain it directly from the former. A simple example of this is where the disclosing party uses a consultant, who provides some of the information to the receiving party. More complex is the situation where the disclosing party discloses information to an independent party, who then passes it on to the receiving party. From a disclosing party's point of view, the phrase 'directly or indirectly' is a useful addition to the definition of confidential information. Receiving parties are sometimes nervous that the phrase may cause them to be bound by obligations of confidentiality in a situation where they received the information in good faith from a third party and the third party did not impose any confidentiality obligations on the receiving party.

Contractual and other relationships

Occasionally, one encounters CDAs that refer to the receiving party having a fiduciary relationship with the disclosing party. The intention of such a reference seems to be to give the disclosing party an opportunity to allege breach of fiduciary duty as well as breach of contract and breach of confidence, and perhaps to clarify that any developments made by the receiving party using the confidential information (e.g., an invention) should be held on trust for the disclosing party. In the author's view references to fiduciary relationships are usually 'over the top' where two independent organisations are holding confidential discussions, and should usually be resisted.

EFFECTIVE DATE

Under English law, the date of execution of an agreement should not be misstated,[3] but it is permissible to provide that the agreement is deemed to have come into effect on a date prior to the date of its execution. The latter date is sometimes known as an effective date or a commencement date.

Backdating a CDA can be problematic. If the information was originally disclosed without any confidentiality undertaking being given, it may have lost the 'necessary quality of confidence' (see discussion in Chapter 2). An alternative analysis, in some cases, is that the information was disclosed in confidence under an oral or implied agreement, and that the later, written

---

[3] In the worst case, this may amount to the offence of forgery, under the Forgery and Counterfeiting Act 1981, s.9(1). The Act specifically mentions the misdating of agreements.

CDA is merely clarifying the extent of the confidentiality obligations already undertaken.

It will usually prejudice or prevent the making of a patent application if the invention disclosed in the patent application was publicly disclosed prior to making the application.[4] Such prejudice will usually not arise where the prior disclosure was made to a small number of people under the terms of a CDA. However, if the disclosure was made in the absence of a written CDA, it may be very difficult to persuade a Patent Office that a subsequently executed CDA is sufficient evidence that the disclosure was made in confidence, even where the written CDA is backdated.

Despite these difficulties, it is not uncommon for a CDA to have an earlier effective date than the date of its execution, or for the definition of confidential information to refer to information disclosed 'prior to, on or after the date of this Agreement'.

DURATION AND TERMINATION OF THE CDA

There are two important 'durations' in a CDA, which should not be confused. Typically, parties may disclose information to one another under a CDA for a period of a few months, before they either: (a) enter into a more substantive agreement; or (b) terminate their discussions. Even though they may have terminated their discussions, and have no intention of making any further confidential disclosures to one another, the CDA will usually be meant to continue for a further period of time. There are therefore two separate periods: the period of disclosure, and the period during which the obligations of confidentiality continue.

Sometimes, CDAs are drafted so as to have a fixed period of disclosure, such as one year from the date of execution of the agreement. If information is disclosed after that period has expired, it will not be subject to the terms of the CDA. However, information that was disclosed prior to the expiry of that period will (if the CDA so provides) continue to be caught by the terms of the CDA for a longer period. Other CDAs are drafted so as to have no fixed period of disclosure, in which case information may be disclosed under the CDA for as long as the obligations of confidentiality continue or (depending on the proper construction of the contract) until one party gives notice to the other party to terminate the agreement.

An example of 'disclosure period' wording follows:

> This agreement shall continue in force for a period of one year from the Effective Date. The obligations set out in clause 2 shall survive the expiry of that one year period, in respect of Confidential Information disclosed prior to such expiry, for a period of [   ].

[4] See further, Anderson: *Technology Transfer – Law, Practice and Precedents*, Butterworths, 2003.

The second 'duration' is the period during which the confidentiality obligations continue, referred to in this section as the obligations period. The obligations period will usually continue for several years (e.g., 5 years), and will usually survive the expiry of any stated period of disclosure.

An example of 'obligations period' wording follows:

> The obligations on the Receiving Party under this Agreement shall continue in force for a period of [5] [10] [15] years from the date of this Agreement.

The parties to a CDA should consider carefully how long the obligations period should continue. This will depend partly on the type of information (e.g., commercial information with a short shelf-life, versus scientific information that may be valuable for many years to come) and on the industry in which the parties are operating (e.g., some computer software may be out of date in a couple of years, whereas information about a process for manufacturing a vaccine may be a valuable secret for a much longer period).

Having reviewed many hundreds of CDAs, the main 'obligation periods' that the author has encountered are the following:

- *one year* (fairly rare);
- *three years* (particularly where the information is primarily business information rather than scientific information);
- *five years* (quite a popular period, sometimes unjustifiably so; sometimes used where the information is computer software);
- *ten years* (quite popular in the biotech industry, although longer periods may sometimes be appropriate); and
- *unlimited* (unpopular with many large companies and with many US companies).

There is a reasonable argument for providing that the obligations of confidentiality should continue until such time as the information falls within one of the exceptions to confidentiality, e.g., that it enters the public domain (see further the discussion of exceptions, later in this chapter). The main argument that is used against this approach is that the receiving party must know when it can finally 'close the file'. As a matter of practice, many companies, particularly in the USA, refuse to accept confidentiality obligations that are unlimited in duration.

Sometimes, such companies will accept an exceptionally long fixed duration, e.g., 15 or 20 years. Where the information is of a technical nature, it may be part of a package with patented information that is protected for 20 years, or longer if improvement patents are filed. In such cases it may be illogical to have an artificial cut-off point in the CDA, particularly if the chosen cut-off point means a shorter period of protection than for patented information. As a practical matter, it may be difficult to reach agreement on a period that strays outside a perceived 'norm' of 5 to 10 years; but if the issue is important enough, received wisdom should be ignored.

The CDA will be deficient if it fails to state any duration for the obligations under it. In such a case, the receiving party might seek to persuade the Court that the CDA can be terminated by either party on reasonable notice and that none of the provisions of the CDA survive termination (i.e., by analogy with *Martin-Baker Aircraft Company* v. *Canadian Flight Equipment Company* [1955] 2 QB 556 and subsequent cases. Although concerned with a patent and know-how licence, that case is often cited as authority for an implied contractual term allowing termination of a range of types of agreement, e.g., distribution agreements, on reasonable notice where no fixed period or general right of termination is provided for).

CONSIDERATION

See the discussion of consideration above, p. 54.

SCOPE AND PURPOSE OF THE CDA

Parties sometimes include in the CDA a brief description of its scope and purpose. There are a number of different reasons for doing this:

(a) to identify the broad subject area of the discussions, and perhaps as a brief aide-memoire for colleagues who are not directly involved in the confidential discussions, but without any particular intention of excluding any subjects from the CDA; or

(b) to limit the obligations under the CDA to information that falls within the defined scope; or

(c) to limit the purposes for which the receiving party may use the information. For example, the receiving party might be permitted to use the information for the purpose of considering whether to enter into a further agreement with the disclosing party, and for no other purpose.

Where the CDA includes a description of its general subject area, a disclosing party would generally wish to have a broader rather than narrower subject area. Take the example of a disclosing party that is developing several business projects. It wishes to hold confidential discussions with another party about one of its projects, and draws up a CDA which defines the subject area of the CDA in terms of that project alone. If the discussions subsequently broaden to other projects, the CDA may not apply to those subsequent discussions. Of course, this problem can be solved, if the parties enter into another CDA or amend the scope of the CDA, but parties sometimes overlook such matters.

An alternative way of describing the subject matter of the discussions, while avoiding the problem referred to above, is to include the description in a definition of the permitted purpose, for which information can be used, as in the following (fictional) example where the description appears in square brackets:

> We are prepared to disclose to you information which we regard as confidential, which you may use for the purpose of considering whether to enter into an agreement with Law Without Fears LLC relating to [the grant of a franchise, on the Island of St Kilda, of our LazyLawyer® business model] (the '**Permitted Purpose**'), provided you accept these terms and conditions:

As a drafting point, a permitted purpose that merely refers to the receiving party 'evaluating' the confidential information may be too general, from the disclosing party's point of view. It would be better to use words similar to those in the above-quoted paragraph or at the very least to add some words, such as 'evaluating the Confidential Information and deciding whether to enter into a further agreement with the Disclosing Party'.

CATEGORIES OF INFORMATION COVERED BY THE AGREEMENT

CDAs sometimes state that the information to be disclosed under the agreement may include commercial, financial, scientific and other types of information. Wording of this kind probably does no harm, provided the list of categories is preceded by words such as 'including without limitation', and may be useful in cases of doubt. However, there would seem to be no legal requirement to specify the types of information, and in many cases this can probably be avoided.

More useful, although often not essential, is wording to clarify that information includes oral and documentary information. The following example also includes wording discussed elsewhere in this section.

> '**Information**' shall include information provided directly or indirectly by ABC to you in oral or documentary form or by way of models, biological or chemical materials or other tangible form or by demonstrations and whether before, on or after the date of this Agreement.

CRITERIA FOR INFORMATION TO BE TREATED AS 'CONFIDENTIAL'

One of the more contentious points that arises when negotiating CDAs is whether orally disclosed information must be confirmed in writing, if it is to be subject to the obligations of the CDA. There are two schools of thought, each of which is legitimate, but very different to one another.

1. Some business people prefer that all information must be confirmed in writing so that in the event of a dispute there will be clear evidence of what information is subject to the confidentiality obligations. Where a party is receiving, and not disclosing, information under a CDA, the attractions of this approach are clear. However, experienced business managers will sometimes adopt this approach irrespective of whether they are disclosing or receiving information. Some people take the view that there should be a consistent company policy on CDAs which should apply both as discloser and recipient.

2. The other approach, preferred by many scientists, is to say that it is unrealistic to take detailed minutes of a discussion so as to identify every item of confidential information. Therefore, the CDA should be drafted so as to cover all disclosures of information, whether or not they are confirmed in writing.

As a lawyer, one's preference may be for the former approach. But if in practice one's client will not take the trouble to confirm oral disclosures in writing, then it may be better to adopt the latter approach. The following example takes the former approach, but can easily be converted into the latter approach by deleting the last couple of lines in the second paragraph.

'**Confidential Information**' shall mean:

(a) in respect of information provided in documentary or by way of a model or in other tangible form, information which at the time of provision is marked or otherwise designated to show expressly or by necessary implication that it is imparted in confidence; and

(b) in respect of information that is imparted orally, any information that the Disclosing Party or its representatives informed the Receiving Party at the time of disclosure was imparted in confidence and which is reduced to writing, marked 'Confidential' and sent to the Receiving Party within 30 days of the original disclosure; and

(c) any copy of any of the foregoing; and

(d) the fact that discussions are taking place between us.

PROVISION OF MATERIALS UNDER A CDA

There are different types of materials. Biological or chemical materials, such as might be disclosed by a biotech company or university, should probably be disclosed under a separate material transfer agreement (MTA). The topics that are usually addressed in MTAs overlap with those to be found in a CDA, but there are also some provisions that are unique to MTAs, including:

- disclaimers of liability and indemnities in relation to the use of the materials;
- restrictions on reproduction of living materials;
- IP ownership and use provisions;
- more detailed reporting obligations; and
- sometimes, provisions for payment for the materials or for delivery costs.

Similar issues may arise where materials or equipment are provided in other areas of science and engineering.

By contrast, materials that merely record the confidential information, e.g., on paper or disk, probably do not merit a separate MTA.

Sometimes, CDAs state that any documents and other materials generated by the recipient that incorporate the disclosing party's confidential information, will belong to the disclosing party. Such a provision, while understandable, can be controversial.

PRINCIPAL OBLIGATIONS WITH RESPECT TO CONFIDENTIAL INFORMATION

The main obligations under a CDA are: not to disclose the information, except as permitted under the CDA and not to use the information, except as permitted under the CDA.

It is surprising how often the latter obligation is omitted, whether by accident or design. The recipient may be able to derive a commercial advantage from internal use of the information without publicly disclosing it, e.g., to develop a product that does not, by itself, incorporate the confidential information.

These main obligations are often accompanied by an obligation to keep the information secret. A general statement of this kind is probably useful, although arguably not essential if there are other provisions that specify what the recipient must do to protect the information, e.g., keep it in a locked filing cabinet. Proving breach of a general obligation of this kind may not be easy.

An example of a clause stating these general obligations follows.

The Receiving Party undertakes to the Disclosing Party:

(a) to keep the Confidential Information secret at all times;
(b) not to disclose it or allow it to be disclosed in whole or in part to any third party without the Disclosing Party's prior written consent; and
(c) not to use it in whole or in part for any purpose except for the Purpose.

EXCEPTIONS

Most CDAs include a list of so-called 'standard' exceptions to the obligations of confidentiality set out in the agreement. Some of these exceptions should be looked at critically by the disclosing party, to see if they are acceptable in the individual case, particularly item (d) below.

A typical set of exceptions might read as follows:

The obligations of confidentiality set out in clause 2 above shall not apply to any Information which the Receiving Party can show by written records:

(a) was known to the Receiving Party before the Information was imparted by the Disclosing Party; or

(b) is in or subsequently comes into the public domain (through no fault on the Receiving Party's part); or

(c) is received by the Receiving Party without restriction on disclosure or use from a third party lawfully entitled to make the disclosure to the Receiving Party without such restrictions; or

(d) is developed by any of the Receiving Party's employees who have not had any direct or indirect access to, or use or knowledge of, the Information imparted by the Disclosing Party; or

(e) is required to be disclosed by an order of any court of competent jurisdiction provided that reasonable efforts shall be used by the Receiving Party to secure a protective order or equivalent over such information and provided further that the Disclosing Party shall be informed as soon as possible and be given an opportunity, if time permits, to make appropriate representations to such court, authority or Stock Exchange to attempt to secure that the information is kept confidential.

Technically, some of these exceptions describe situations where the information should not be regarded as having the necessary quality of confidence, while exception (e) above describes situations where, although the information is confidential, the obligations of confidentiality should be waived. Some drafters prefer to deal with these situations separately.

The above wording throws up a number of drafting issues, including the following phrases.

'Obligations of confidentiality'

Some CDAs, particularly those drafted in the USA, refer to 'obligations of confidentiality and non-use', presumably because of a concern that restrictions on use of the information are not obligations of confidentiality. The author considers it unlikely that an English court would impose such a narrow construction on the phrase 'obligations of confidentiality'.

'By written records'

In the above example this phrase qualifies all of the exceptions in (a) to (e) above. In some CDAs, such a qualification is included for some but not all of the exceptions. Other phrases, such as 'satisfactory evidence' or 'written evidence' are sometimes used and are less satisfactory. A witness statement, prepared after proceedings had been commenced, and asserting that the recipient already knew the information before it was disclosed by the disclosing party, might amount to written evidence but it would not be as persuasive as a contemporaneous written record.

'In the public domain'

This expression is used in different ways by different people. Some people take the view that it means both: (a) known to, or accessible by, the public; and (b) not subject to any legal restrictions, e.g., a patent, which would prevent it from being used by the public. In the context of CDAs, (b) is probably less relevant (if there are any IP rights, these can be used separately to prevent misuse of the information). Arguably, from a receiving party's perspective, the phrase should be replaced by one such as 'publicly known'.

'Direct or indirect access to'

From a disclosing party's perspective, exception (d) above may be the most controversial of the exceptions. Sometimes, disclosing parties are not willing to accept that the receiving party can learn the information then independently develop the same information. From a receiving party's perspective, particularly in large organisations, it may be possible that someone, somewhere, in another part of the organisation, has come up with the same information. The issue should be whether they did so in light of any information from the disclosing party. Where an exception such as (d) is included, the disclosing party may wish to have the references to 'access' drafted as broadly as possible, hence the phrase 'direct or indirect'. An example of indirect access might be that Mr X received the information from the disclosing party. He does not disclose that information to his colleague Dr Y, but discusses with Dr Y the work that Dr Y is doing in a similar field to that of the disclosing party's information. Whether consciously or subconsciously, Mr X steers Dr Y in a particular direction based on his knowledge of the disclosing party's information.

'Court of competent jurisdiction'

It may be appropriate to extend the reference to courts to include other bodies, such as competition authorities (e.g., the European Commission) and stock exchanges on which the receiving party is listed. A practical issue is whether the disclosing party wants the receiving party to make any applications to have the information treated in a confidential manner, or prefers to make such applications itself, where this is possible.

SECURITY PRECAUTIONS

Depending on the sensitivity of the confidential information, it may be appropriate to require the recipient to comply with detailed security precautions, in addition to having the general obligations of confidentiality referred to above.

If a simple statement is all that is thought desirable, it might be along the following lines:

> The Receiving Party undertakes to take proper and all reasonable measures to ensure the confidentiality of the Confidential Information.

An alternative, general approach is to say that the receiving party must treat the information in the same way that it treats its own confidential information. This approach is more subjective than the words quoted above, and presumably will only be acceptable to a disclosing party if it is confident that the receiving party's procedures are adequate.

If more detailed security precautions are required, the CDA might include provisions to address the following issues:

(a) keeping the information in a locked cabinet to which only named individuals have access;

(b) keeping a log of all occasions on which the information is accessed;

(c) prohibiting the making of copies;

(d) keeping a log of all copies made and to whom they are provided;

(e) requiring all copies to have a unique identification number; and

(f) limiting access to the information to named individuals or to individuals who have signed a confidentiality undertaking (i.e., one that has been specially prepared for this information and not just a general employee confidentiality undertaking).

DISCLOSURE TO EMPLOYEES, ADVISERS AND OTHERS

Where the receiving party is a company, someone within the company needs to have access to the information, as a company cannot perceive information. Unless the information is exceptionally sensitive, it is normal in CDAs to allow the receiving party to disclose the information to employees who need to know it in connection with the purpose for which the information was disclosed. Usually, this is conditional upon the employee being bound by obligations of confidentiality, but the exact form of this condition varies from agreement to agreement. It might, for example, be couched in the following terms.

The Receiving Party undertakes to permit access to the Confidential Information only to those of the Receiving Party's directors and employees who reasonably need access to the Confidential Information for the Purpose, and on the conditions that such directors and employees shall have:

(a) entered into legally binding confidentiality obligations to the Receiving Party on terms equivalent to those set out in this Agreement (and such obligations extend to the Confidential Information);

(b) been informed of the Disclosing Party's interest in the Confidential Information and the terms of this Agreement; and

(c) been instructed to treat the Confidential Information as secret and confidential in accordance with the provisions of this Agreement.

The above wording raises a number of drafting and policy issues, including:

1. The wording refers only to directors and employees. Sometimes receiving parties ask for it to include consultants. As a practical matter, a disclosing party may be concerned that consultants are not under the control of the receiving party to the same extent as employees and directors. Some disclosing parties take the view that consultants should sign a separate CDA with the disclosing party. Similar issues arise where the receiving party requests that such wording extend to employees of its affiliates (see earlier discussion, pp. 55–57).

2. Arguably the best protection for the disclosing party is for the receiving party's employees to sign a CDA directly with the disclosing party, or (nearly as good) to sign a CDA with the employer that has been specially prepared in connection with the main CDA between disclosing party and receiving party. But these measures are often regarded by the parties as unnecessary as long as the employee has general obligations of confidentiality towards his employer.

3. The above wording takes a fairly cautious approach to the issue of employees having confidentiality obligations towards the employer. English case law on employees' duties of confidentiality seems to suggest that it is important for the employer to draw the employee's attention to any information that is regarded as particularly sensitive; the employer may not be able just to rely on wording in the employment contract that requires the employee to treat all information learned in the course of his employment as confidential. Hence the detailed wording of paragraphs (a) to (c) above.

4. Many CDAs are between people or organisations based in different countries. One should not assume that the obligations of confidentiality that are implied in English employment law will apply in all countries, nor that it will be common practice for companies to have written confidentiality agreements with their employees in other countries.

It is becoming increasingly common for CDAs to refer to disclosures to a party's external advisers, such as lawyers, accountants and financial brokers.

RESPONSIBILITY FOR EMPLOYEES, ETC.

If an employee (or, more usually, an ex-employee) of the receiving party breaches the obligations set out in the CDA, the question arises as to whether his or her employer (the receiving party) should be responsible for bringing an action for breach of confidence against the employee and, as a slightly different question, whether the employer should be obliged to bring such an action. A further question is whether the receiving party should be liable for or indemnify the disclosing party against any loss suffered as a result of the employee's misuse or disclosure of the information.

These issues are not always dealt with in detail in a typical CDA. If action has to be taken against the employee, it is probably more appropriate that the employer should take it rather than the disclosing party, particularly if the employee has not entered into any agreement with the disclosing party. It is probably less controversial to refer to the receiving party being 'responsible' for taking action against the employee than to say directly that the receiving party must do so or that the receiving party is liable for any breach by his employees. The following wording slightly fudges the issue, but this may not be a bad thing to do:

> The Receiving Party shall be responsible for ensuring that the Receiving Party's directors and employees comply with the provisions of this Agreement.

An alternative approach can be seen in the following wording:

> The Recipient shall be responsible for any breach of the terms of this Agreement by the Recipient or any of the Related Parties and the Recipient agrees, at its sole expense, to take all reasonable measures (including but not limited to court proceedings) to restrain the Related Parties from prohibited or unauthorised disclosure or use of the Confidential Information.

REPORTING AND AUDITING

Where the receiving party intends to conduct some feasibility studies or other work using the disclosing party's information, the disclosing party may wish to provide in the CDA that the receiving party will provide it with a copy of any such report and/or that disclosing party has a veto or right of review prior to publication over any such report.

As a separate issue, the disclosing party may wish to include some rights of audit over the use that the receiving party has made of the confidential information. Such provisions are relatively rare in routine CDAs.

INTELLECTUAL PROPERTY

Sometimes, CDAs provide that any intellectual property that may exist in the confidential information remains the property of the disclosing party, as in the following example:

> The Receiving Party acknowledges and agrees that the property and copyright in Confidential Information disclosed to it by the Disclosing Party, including any documents, files and other items containing any Confidential Information, belongs to the Disclosing Party.

Arguments sometimes arise as to whether documents generated by the receiving party, which incorporate the disclosing party's information (e.g., a Board report), should belong to the disclosing party.

Similarly, CDAs sometimes provide that any intellectual property generated by the receiving party using the disclosing party's information will belong to the disclosing party. Such provisions can be controversial. An example of such a provision follows:

> Any intellectual property arising from any evaluation of the Technology conducted hereunder shall belong beneficially to the Disclosing Party.

More commonly encountered, and generally regarded as less controversial, is a provision that states that the disclosing party is not granting any licence to its intellectual property by virtue of the CDA. The reason why this is uncontroversial is probably because it is unlikely that either party would expect that any licence was being granted, under a typical CDA. Provisions such as the following are therefore usually fairly harmless boilerplate, at least under English law. Nevertheless, provisions of this kind are quite often seen:

> No right or licence to any intellectual property of any of the Developers or to any information disclosed under this Agreement is granted or implied by virtue of this Agreement.

RETURN OF INFORMATION

CDAs usually provide that the receiving party will return the confidential information, including any copies that it has made, to the disclosing party upon request and in any event upon termination of the agreement.

An exception is usually made to allow a single copy of the documents or other materials, on which the confidential information is recorded, to be retained in the receiving party's 'legal files' for the purpose of ensuring compliance with the terms of the CDA. Where the receiving party does not have a legal department, it may be open to question what the expression 'legal files' really means. Without this single copy, it may be difficult for the receiving party to know whether it has been in breach of the CDA.

LAW AND JURISDICTION

Where the CDA is between parties from different jurisdictions, the question arises as to which law should apply to the CDA, and which courts should have exclusive or non-exclusive jurisdiction.

While the disclosing party may generally prefer to litigate in its own jurisdiction, it should bear in mind that the most likely proceedings for breach of a CDA may be an urgent application for an interim injunction to prevent disclosure of the information. Such actions are usually best brought in the receiving party's jurisdiction, not least because of the difficulty and delay involved in trying to enforce an interim judgment that was obtained in a different jurisdiction.

Thus, the disclosing party may prefer to state that its own country's courts will have non-exclusive, rather than exclusive, jurisdiction.

If an injunction application is brought in the receiving party's home territory, the next question for the disclosing party is whether the court should be asked to apply its own local law or the law of the disclosing party's home territory. In other words, what should be the law of the contract? It may lead to a more predictable result if the former is chosen. In such cases, the disclosing party should be advised to take advice on the effect of the CDA under such laws prior to signing it. In practice, clients often consider that it is not commercially justified to take local legal advice on a CDA, particularly when the other party is based in a common law jurisdiction.

Whatever the merits of this approach, parties sometimes agree to leave the law and jurisdiction of their CDA unstated, rather than spend a great deal of time trying to negotiate these matters.

An example of a simple clause providing for English law and non-exclusive English jurisdiction follows.

This Agreement shall be governed by and construed in accordance with English law and shall be subject to the non-exclusive jurisdiction of the English courts.

ENTITLEMENT TO INJUNCTION

A practice has arisen of including a provision stating that the disclosing party may obtain an injunction if the receiving party breaches the terms of the CDA. It seems that this practice has migrated from North America. An example of such a clause follows.

> The Recipient agrees that disclosure or use of the Confidential Information without the consent of the Disclosing Party would cause irreparable harm to the Disclosing Party, and that in the event of such disclosure or use, the Disclosing Party shall be entitled to, in addition to any other remedies available to it, equitable relief in the nature of an injunction or specific performance.

The above wording fails to take into account the fact that, under English law, injunctions are an equitable remedy and at the discretion of the court. The best that can be said for it is that the recipient may be estopped from opposing an injunction where it has agreed to such terms, although even this may not be clear under English law.

A less absolute form of words can be seen in the following example:

> Without prejudice to any other rights or remedies that the DISCLOSER may have, the RECIPIENT acknowledges and agrees that
>
> (a) damages would not be an adequate remedy for any breach by it of the provisions of this Agreement;
> (b) the DISCLOSER shall be entitled to [seek] the remedies of injunction, specific performance and other equitable relief for any threatened or actual breach of the provisions of this Agreement; and
> (c) no proof of special damages shall be necessary for the enforcement of this Agreement.

The traditional wisdom among English intellectual property lawyers was that provisions of this kind were of limited value, and might be counter-productive if judges took offence at what might be seen as an attempt to tell them how to exercise their discretion. As such provisions become more 'standard', this concern is probably no longer so significant. This provision is probably more appropriate for a detailed CDA than for the very brief kind of CDA.

OTHER LEGAL RELATIONSHIPS AND REMEDIES

This book has already referred to the legal relationships and remedies that may arise under general law or by contract, for breach of confidence. Occasionally, CDAs are drafted in an imaginative way, to include references to other types of relationship and remedy. The author has occasionally seen references in CDAs to the following phrases.

Utmost good faith

Obligations of 'utmost good faith' arise in certain types of contract, particularly insurance contracts, but not in most types of contract. The obligation requires a higher level of disclosure of information between the parties than would be the case for most types of contract. Occasionally, such obligations have been included in CDAs, although this is far from common. More usually, parties disclaim any warranty that the information they have disclosed is complete or accurate.

Fiduciary-type duties

The possible inclusion of references to fiduciary relationships between the parties has already been mentioned (see p. 58). Variations on this approach are sometimes seen, e.g., where the CDA includes references to the receiving party having an obligation to act in the best interests of the disclosing party, or to hold any developments made by it using the confidential information on trust for the disclosing party. Some of these obligations may arise without the need for such wording, by virtue of the relationship of confidence between the parties. In any event, express provisions of this kind usually seem 'over the top' for most CDAs. In the case of CDAs where the disclosing party is a company, and the receiving party is a director of that company, such express obligations may be a helpful reminder to the director of his duties that arise by virtue of being a director.

Relationship of privilege

The following wording comes from a CDA drafted by a US lawyer. It seems to be attempting to argue that the disclosure of information under the CDA does not amount to a waiver of privilege, under relevant US laws. The author has not seen any such provision in a CDA drafted by an English lawyer.

> To the extent that any Confidential Information may include material or information that is subject to the attorney–client privilege, work product doctrine or any other applicable privilege concerning any pending or threatened action, suit, proceeding, investigation, arbitration or dispute, Recipient understands and agrees that it has a commonality of interest with respect to such matters and it is their desire, intention and mutual understanding that the sharing of such material or information is not intended to, and shall not, waive or diminish in any way the confidentiality of such material or information or its continued protection under the attorney–client privilege, work product doctrine or other applicable privilege. Any Confidential Information that is entitled to protection under the attorney–client privilege, work product doctrine or other applicable privilege shall remain entitled to such protection under such privileges, under this Agreement and under the joint defense doctrine. Nothing in this Agreement obligates any party to reveal material or information subject to the attorney–client privilege, work product doctrine or any other applicable privilege.

REPRESENTATIONS, WARRANTIES AND DISCLAIMERS

Liability and indemnities

Usually, CDAs will seek to exclude liability for the accuracy and completeness of information provided, as in the following example:

> This Agreement shall not be construed so as to require the Disclosing Party to disclose any Confidential Information to the Receiving Party. No warranty or representation, express or implied, is given as to the accuracy, efficacy, completeness, capabilities or safety of any materials or information provided under this Agreement.

A rather more detailed clause, along the same lines, follows:

> It is acknowledged and agreed that:
>
> 1. In respect of the Confidential Information and any other information supplied to the Investor or its advisers, neither the Developers nor any of their respective directors, employees or agents:
>
>   (a) makes (nor is authorised to make) any representation nor gives (nor is authorised to give) any warranty (express or implied) and (without limiting the foregoing disclaimers) no representation or warranty is made or is to be implied that the information will remain unchanged; nor
>   (b) shall have any responsibility or liability for its accuracy or completeness or for any other matter concerning the Technology or the Developers. The Investor must make its own independent assessment of the Technology and the Developers and rely on its own judgment in reaching any conclusion.
>
> 2. Nothing contained in this Agreement shall compel the Developers to provide the Investor with all or any information relating to the Developers or the Technology requested by the Investor and that the Developers shall be entitled at their discretion without giving any reason therefor to decline or continue to supply the Investor with any of such information.
> 3. No documents or information made available to the investor or its advisers will constitute an offer or invitation or form the basis of any contract.

Sometimes, receiving parties seek to include in the CDA a warranty that the disclosing party is entitled to disclose the information and grant to the receiving party the right to use it in the manner anticipated by the agreement. It is ultimately a commercial question as to whether such a provision is included, but receiving parties sometimes accept the argument, when put to them, that it is not appropriate to include warranties in a CDA for an early 'look-see' at the information. Detailed warranties of this kind can be negotiated in any subsequent agreement between the parties and, if necessary, can be backdated to cover information disclosed under the CDA.

Sometimes, parties seek to include indemnities in a CDA, e.g., a party that breaches the terms of the CDA must indemnify the other party against any losses that it may suffer as a result. Such provisions are relatively rare in simple CDAs.

It is very rare indeed to see exemption clauses in CDAs. For example, the clauses that someone sees in other types of agreement – liability for direct losses limited to a fixed amount, and indirect and consequential losses excluded – are rarely seen.

ASSIGNMENT

Although clauses dealing with assignment are sometimes seen in CDAs, they should be treated with caution. When advising the disclosing party, the following points might be made.

1. Should the receiving party be allowed to extend the agreement so that a party that was not originally intended to receive the information may now do so, at the discretion of the receiving party? Would it not be better for the disclosing party to enter into a new CDA with the new party, if the need arises and if the disclosing party is happy to disclose its information to that party?
2. Even if it is appropriate to allow the receiving party to assign its rights under the agreement, should it not continue to be bound by the obligations under the CDA (i.e., both assignor and assignee should be bound to comply with the terms of the CDA)?

These points may make a typical assignment clause inappropriate in many cases.

OBLIGATIONS TO ENTER INTO FURTHER AGREEMENTS

Sometimes, CDAs state that the parties have no obligation to enter into any further agreements. In many situations in which CDAs are used, at least under English law, this is probably a 'for the avoidance of doubt' provision that does no harm, but is unlikely to be needed. It may be more necessary under some other countries' laws. For example, it is understood that under some Continental European countries' laws, signing a letter of intent or heads of agreement may result in the parties having an obligation of good faith to one another in subsequent negotiations, such that a party may not unilaterally withdraw from the negotiations without good reason. It may also be (although the author has no direct experience of this) that signing a CDA could be regarded in a similar light to a letter of intent. Whatever the reasons, provisions such as the following are often seen in CDAs:

> This Agreement shall not be construed so as to grant the Receiving Party any licence or rights other than as expressly set out herein in respect of the Confidential Information nor so as to require the parties to enter into any further agreements.

It will be noted that the above wording specifically mentions licences, which have already been mentioned in the context of intellectual property – see p. 70.

EXCLUSIVITY AND NON-COMPETITION OBLIGATIONS

Sometimes, a disclosing party will ask for a 'stand-still' provision to be included in the CDA. By 'stand-still' the client generally either means one of the following two provisions.

1. A provision that prohibits the receiving party from investing in the disclosing party or trading in its shares for a defined period. The argument used for such a provision is that the receiving party will learn valuable secrets about the disclosing party, such that it should be treated as an 'insider' for the purposes of insider-dealing laws, and therefore should not be in a position to profit from this knowledge. For example, if a high-tech company discloses information to a multinational company in order to interest the latter in taking a licence to the high-tech company's technology, then without such a provision the multinational can simply buy the high-tech company (if its shares are publicly traded) rather than buy the licence. This is a specialist area of corporate law and beyond the scope of this book.
2. A provision that prevents the receiving party from investing in a competing enterprise for a defined period. Again, the argument is that the receiving party will learn valuable secrets about the disclosing party's business and (in the case of high-tech companies) technology, and should not be free to take that information to a rival company and help that rival grow at the expense of the disclosing party.

An example of the latter type of provision follows:

> ABC undertakes to each of the Developers that, for a period of 2 years from the date of this Agreement, it shall not, directly or indirectly, make any investment in, or otherwise be involved in controlling or managing, any company involved in developing new or improved products or processes relating to the use of [widgets in microprocessors], without the prior written consent of Discloser.

Any provisions that restrict a party from doing something, or grant exclusive rights to a party, should be considered in the light of applicable competition laws. Restrictive provisions are not usually encountered in simple CDAs. The main exception to this is probably the situation where parties enter into an exclusive negotiation agreement that includes confidentiality terms. Similarly, parties sometimes enter into a letter of intent or term sheet that is stated to be non-binding, except for its confidentiality and exclusivity provisions.

'EXTRA-STRONG' PROVISIONS

Sometimes clients express concern that the information that they are about to disclose is very important and therefore the CDA should be as protective of the disclosing party as it can possibly be. The first question to ask the client in such a situation is whether the information should be disclosed. See further the discussion of strategic issues, in Chapter 5.

If the client is insistent on going ahead with the disclosure, it may be appropriate to include what might be called some 'extra-strong' provisions in the CDA. Such provisions will usually not change the basic obligations of the parties, but they may help to clarify the nature of the receiving party's obligations, and give added emphasis to the seriousness with which the disclosing party views the matter. Where the information to be disclosed is of a scientific or technical nature, the extra-strong provisions might include the following:

> Without prejudice to the generality of the foregoing, the Receiving Party undertakes that, except as may be permitted in any future written agreement between the Parties:
>
> (a) the Receiving Party shall not make any inventions or developments using or based on the Disclosing Party's Confidential Information, and if any such inventions or developments are made, the Receiving Party shall assign all rights in them to the Disclosing Party or its nominee;
>
> (b) the Receiving Party shall not attempt to replicate the Disclosing Party's Confidential Information nor to investigate detailed aspects of the Disclosing Party's Confidential Information that were not disclosed by the Disclosing Party; and
>
> (c) the Receiving Party shall not use the Disclosing Party's Confidential Information directly or indirectly to procure a commercial benefit to the Receiving Party or a commercial disbenefit to the Disclosing Party (including without limitation to support any patent applications being made by the Receiving Party or to obtain or submit evidence to support an allegation of patent infringement).

COSTS

Very few CDAs include provisions on the subject of the costs of preparing and negotiating the agreement. Where such provisions are seen, they tend to provide that each party bears its own costs, as in the following example:

77

The Developers are not under any obligation to reimburse any costs and expenses which the Investor or its advisers may incur in connection with the discussions relating to the Investment or the review of the Technology unless expressly agreed in writing.

SIGNING AND EXCHANGING THE AGREEMENT

There is no established convention as to how CDAs are signed and exchanged. They are treated like many other types of commercial agreement. Typically, CDAs are signed at short notice to allow the parties to begin their discussions. In such cases, the CDA is sometimes signed at the start of the first meeting between the parties (one of them having brought it to the meeting); sometimes they are signed and exchanged by fax prior to the meeting.

CHAPTER 7

Special situations and relationships

COMMERCIAL SETTLEMENT AGREEMENTS

Most disputes that arise under commercial contracts are resolved by negoti-ation rather than litigation. The terms on which a dispute is resolved are often recorded in a written agreement, known as a settlement agreement.

Parties will often include in their settlement agreement some confidentiality provisions. Such provisions typically address some or all of the following issues:

1. The terms of settlement must be kept confidential.
2. Sometimes, the parties agree the wording of a press release.
3. Some 'standard' exceptions to confidentiality are included in the agreement.

For example, if one or both parties are listed on a stock exchange, they may need to disclose information concerning the settlement to a listing authority or stock exchange. If they are listed on a US stock exchange, and if the settlement agreement is 'material', they may need to file a copy of the agreement with the Securities and Exchange Commission. If so, they will probably wish to agree on which sensitive provisions of the agreement are to be 'redacted', i.e., deleted, on the version of the agreement that appears on the public register.

CONTRACTS OF EMPLOYMENT

There is a considerably large amount of case law on the extent to which an employee owes confidentiality obligations to his employer. As discussed earlier in this book (see Chapter 4), the cases are not entirely consistent with one another, but it seems that the obligations:

(a) are different for an ex-employee than for a current employee;
(b) differ according to whether the information is:
   (i) part of the employee's general skill and knowledge, or
   (ii) a 'trade secret' of the employer (trade secrets being the

highest category, in respect of which employers are entitled to the most protection).

It seems that the obligations of the employee can to a limited extent be increased, or at least clarified, by means of suitably worded written confidentiality agreements and procedures that draw to the employee's attention any information that the employer considers to be particularly sensitive.

CDAs between employer and employee should not seek to impose obligations on the employee that are not permitted under this case law, as this may cause the offending provision to be struck down. If the offending provision cannot easily be separated from other provisions, then other provisions may also be struck down, i.e., applying the 'blue-pencil' test.

The following suggestions are made with a view to maximising the protection given to an employer under a CDA between employer and employee. The CDA should include specific provisions that make clear the following points:

1. Identify any general categories of information that the employer regards as particularly sensitive.
2. In the case of high-tech companies and any other type of company where this is relevant, include in the CDA an acknowledgement by the employee that the company's confidential information is an important asset of the company that requires protection to the fullest extent.
3. The CDA is not to be interpreted as placing restrictions on the use of the employee's general skill and knowledge, after leaving the employment.
4. Specify any procedures that the employee must follow for disclosing inventions and other intellectual property to the employer (taking into consideration the Patents Act 1977, ss.39–43, as amended).
5. Try to draft the CDA in plain English, so as to make its terms as clear as possible to all employees.
6. Include in the CDA the name of an individual who may be consulted if the employee is in any doubt as to whether the employer regards a particular item of information as confidential.

CONFIDENTIALITY AGREEMENTS WITH INVESTORS

CDAs with investors tend to include many of the provisions that are found in CDAs between companies. But CDAs with investors sometimes have unique features, including those set out below.

1. The period of the confidentiality obligations tends to be fairly short, e.g., one to three years. Much will depend, though, on the nature of the information being disclosed.

2. Some 'City' institutions, e.g., brokers and sponsors, are not willing to have very onerous confidentiality obligations. One of the arguments used is that they have to be free to disclose information to the regulatory authorities (e.g., particularly if they are a company's 'sponsor' with the Stock Exchange).

3. It may be appropriate to clarify in the CDA the capacity in which the 'investor' is receiving the information, e.g., as principal or as agent for another person.

4. It may be appropriate for the party disclosing the information to clarify that it makes no representation as to the accuracy or completeness of the information. Generally, any investment decision should be on the basis of the terms of an investment agreement, including any representation and warranties that it contains, rather than on the basis of a preliminary CDA.

5. Given that some investment agreements require the company receiving the investment to bear the investor's legal costs, it may be desirable, from the prospective investee's point of view, that each party bears its own costs in connection with the CDA.

In some cases it may be possible and appropriate to include non-competition obligations on the investor, e.g., that if it does not invest in the other party to the CDA, it will not invest in a company in the same sector for a defined period, e.g., one or two years.

CONTRACTS GOVERNED BY OFFICIAL SECRECY RULES

Contractors who provide goods or services to a UK government department are sometimes required to accept special confidentiality obligations. The contractor's employees and subcontractors may also be required to accept confidentiality obligations. The basis of such obligations may be:

(a) contractual obligations that the contractor has agreed with the government department; and/or

(b) obligations arising under the Official Secrets Acts 1911–1989 (the Official Secrets Acts).

Contractually-assumed confidentiality obligations

There are various sets of 'standard' contract conditions that UK government departments seek to include in their contracts with commercial organisations. Two of the main sets of conditions are:

(a) GC/STORES/1 – Standard Conditions of Government Contracts for Stores Purchase; and

(b)   DEFCONS – Defence Conditions of Contract.

A useful overview of some of the main sets of conditions in use can be found on the MOD acquisitions website (**www.ams.mod.uk**).

These standard conditions should not be confused with those used by overseas governments. For example, the US Department of Defense also has sets of standard terms known as DFARS (Defense Federal Acquisition Regulations), further details of which can be found at the US Department of Defense website (**www.acq.osd.mil/dpap/dfars/**).

On the subject of confidentiality, two important UK government contract conditions are:

(a)   DEFCON 531 (Edn 10/97) – Disclosure of Information; and
(b)   DEFCON 659 (Edn 9/97) – Security Measures.

An index of UK DEFCONS, with links to the text of each DEFCON, may be found on the MOD acquisitions website (**www.ams.mod.uk**).

DEFCON 531 deals with ordinary confidentiality obligations, and raises no special issues. DEFCON 659 has some rather strict provisions that, in summary, require the contractor:

(a)   to ensure that its employees who work on the contract are aware that the Official Secrets Acts apply to them;
(b)   if required by the government, to ensure that its employees sign a statement acknowledging that they are bound by the Official Secrets Acts;
(c)   not to allow confidential information to be disclosed to unauthorised personnel;
(d)   to take all reasonable steps to protect confidential information;
(e)   to maintain certain records, and provide these to the government, on request;
(f)   to allow the government to audit the contractor's compliance with the security obligations;
(g)   to obtain the government's prior approval of any sub-contracts which would involve disclosure of confidential information; and
(h)   to incorporate the contract terms set out in an Appendix to DEFCON 659 in any such sub-contract. (The Appendix largely repeats the conditions set out in the main part of DEFCON 659.)

Paragraph 8 of DEFCON 659 allows the government department to terminate the contract if the contractor is in breach of its confidentiality obligations.

A contractor could address items (a) and (b) above by requiring relevant employees (and, according to the terms of DEFCON 659, relevant directors) to sign a special confidentiality agreement. An example of some simple contract terms dealing with the Official Secrets Acts, that might be included in a confidentiality agreement with employees, is included in paragraphs 7 and 8 of Precedent C at the end of this book. Please note that those paragraphs refer to information relating to 'defence'. As will be seen, below, in addition to information concerning defence, the Official Secrets Acts cover various other categories of information, including information relating to security, intelligence, or international relations. Depending on the subject matter of the contract with the government department, it may be appropriate to modify or expand those references in the precedents, so as to mention any other relevant categories of information.

Obligations arising under the Official Secrets Acts

The Official Secrets Acts establish criminal offences associated with the disclosure by a person of certain categories of 'official information'. In essence, official information is information that has come into a person's possession through an authorised or unauthorised disclosure by a crown servant or government contractor. The categories of information are:

- security and intelligence;
- defence;
- international relations;
- foreign confidences;
- information which might lead to the commission of a crime;
- the special investigation powers under the Interception of Communications Act 1985 and the Security Service Act 1989.

There are also offences associated with the disclosure of information useful to an enemy and failure to take reasonable care to protect official information or to return it to an appropriate body when required to do so.

The Official Secrets Act 1989, which replaces section 2 of the 1911 Act, may be found on the HM Stationery Office website (**www.hmso.gov.uk**). Unfortunately, the Official Secrets Acts 1911–1939 are not yet available on this website.

A person may be bound by obligations under the Official Secrets Acts, even though the obligations have not been drawn to his attention. The traditional practice of asking a person to 'sign' the Official Secrets Acts (or, more accurately, to sign a statement acknowledging that he is bound by the Acts) is not strictly necessary for the Acts to apply. The purpose of signing such a statement is simply to draw the obligations to the person's attention.

CHAPTER 8

Managing the flow of information

KEEPING RECORDS OF DISCLOSURES, COPYING, ETC.

The subject of record-keeping has already been discussed (see pp. 48–49). Whether or not it is a requirement of the CDA that oral disclosures of information should be confirmed in writing, it is a good idea to keep a record of what information has been provided, received, copied, distributed, etc. This will generally assist an innocent party to bring or defend litigation over the CDA.

APPOINTING A COORDINATOR

It may be desirable to appoint someone, e.g., a senior secretary or member of the client's commercial department, to make sure that a CDA has been signed prior to disclosure, to oversee the disclosure and receipt of information under the CDA, monitor any deadlines (e.g., the expiry date of the CDA), where appropriate keep a log of which employees have received the confidential information of an external party, and take any other steps thought desirable, e.g., recording details of the CDA in a contracts database (as to which, see below, p. 85).

MAKING EMPLOYEES AND OTHERS AWARE OF THEIR OBLIGATIONS

There is both a practical and legal need to make employees aware of their obligations in respect of CDAs. Case law in the employment field suggests that it is as important to make employees aware of the practical aspects of their obligations as it is to have them sign a written CDA with their employer (see further, Chapter 4). Those practical aspects include identifying any third-party confidential information, perhaps labelling it clearly as confidential, informing any employee who receives third-party information that it must be kept confidential and not used except as permitted under the CDA with the third party. In some cases it may be appropriate to provide a copy of that CDA to the employee.

MAINTAINING EFFECTIVE SECURITY MEASURES

Organisations are sometimes rather casual about their treatment of confidential information. For example, it may be kept in a lockable cupboard, but the cupboard is not always locked. Or too many people have access to the key. Sometimes, materials are lost when there is an office move, and they end up on a skip somewhere. It may be important to devise appropriate security procedures and then make sure, by instruction and periodic checks, that people are actually complying with the procedures.

AVOIDING OVER-DISCLOSURE

If a party's confidential information is only likely to be of interest to a limited number of people or organisations, and the information is then disclosed to most or all of those people or organisations, there is a risk that the information may lose its quality of confidence, even if every disclosure was made under the terms of a CDA. While such situations may be very rare, they should not be overlooked entirely.

CONTRACTS DATABASES

Some organisations enter into large numbers of CDAs, to enable them to discuss potential business ventures with large numbers of organisations. It can be difficult to keep track of if party A wants to talk to party B:

- Is there already a CDA in place between them?
- Has it expired?
- Does it cover the type of discussions that are contemplated (e.g., is its scope wide enough)?
- Are its terms suitable for the discussions that are now contemplated?
- Are there any procedures that have to be followed (e.g., confirming oral disclosures in writing)?

Maintaining a database of CDAs, which includes brief details of the terms of each CDA, can be of assistance in situations such as the one outlined above. Many commercially available database programs can be adapted for this purpose.

CHAPTER 9

Conclusions

Some commercial clients regard confidentiality agreements (CDAs) as routine documents that do not require careful consideration or legal advice. Their reasons for holding this view vary. For example:

(a) CDAs are all the same;
(b) no one ever sues for breach of a CDA;
(c) CDAs are symbolic – the fact of signing them is more important than their content; or
(d) they are not important enough to spend time in negotiating them.

Other clients take a more circumspect view, particularly if they have been involved in litigation in respect of a breach-of-confidence matter.

Most of the terms of CDAs are becoming fairly standardised (even though the precise wording may differ), particularly in Anglo-American legal practice, but many organisations seem to prefer a few variations on the standard. In the author's experience, when reviewing a typical, well-drafted CDA, it is usual to find that perhaps 90 per cent of the document is standard. The remaining 10 per cent is rarely the same from CDA to CDA. As is discussed in more detail earlier (see Chapter 6), the areas that differ typically include one or more of the following:

(a) whether orally disclosed information must be identified as confidential at the time of disclosure, and whether orally disclosed information must be confirmed in writing;
(b) whether written information must be marked as confidential;
(c) the duration of the confidentiality obligations;
(d) the law and jurisdiction of the CDA;
(e) whether the recipient can retain one copy of the confidential materials in its legal files; and
(f) whether the obligations (and rights of disclosure) extend to affiliates of the recipient.

Items (a) and (b) above are policy issues; clients' views vary. Item (c) should depend on the nature of the information, but typical periods are three, five and ten years. In international contracts, item (d) is sometimes left unstated

– this is a pragmatic commercial solution rather than one that stands up to much legal scrutiny. Item (e) is usually uncontroversial once discussed – i.e., the CDA will often allow one copy to be retained in a party's legal files for the purposes of ensuring compliance with the provisions of the CDA. Item (f) is sometimes not considered carefully enough (see the discussion at pp. 55–58).

The appropriate level of detail to be included in a CDA will depend partly on the level of sensitivity of the information. It is possible to draft a satisfactory CDA, covering the basics, which fits on one side of a sheet of A4, typed in 12-point size, and which is sufficient for many situations where confidential information is disclosed. But conciseness is not always the primary objective.

The practical protection given to confidential information in England and Wales under written CDAs depends on several factors, of which the top four may typically be:

(a) the general law of confidence under English law;
(b) the contractual terms of the CDA;
(c) learning of the proposed breach of confidence before it happens; and
(d) acting quickly enough to get an injunction to restrain public disclosure.

When it comes to protecting commercial information, written confidentiality obligations are just one part of the overall picture. Other factors may include:

(a) deciding whether to disclose the information, how much to disclose and to whom;
(b) protecting the information by other means, including patents and copyright; and
(c) quickly making use of the information, e.g., by getting one's products or services onto the market ahead of one's competitors.

We hope that the information contained in this book will assist you to protect your, or your client's, commercial interests.

Precedents

A   Routine one-way confidentiality agreement

B   Routine two-way confidentiality agreement

C   Additional clauses that may be suitable in particular situations

D   Extra-strong clause to be added to standard CDA

E   Confidentiality clause in settlement agreement

F   Confidentiality clauses in contract of employment (technology-based company)

G   Confidentiality agreement with auditor of royalties

H   Very short and simple one-way confidentiality agreement (not for use where information is valuable)

I   Letter certifying destruction of confidential information

J   Confidentiality undertaking by researcher to a third party company

Precedents

A ROUTINE ONE-WAY CONFIDENTIALITY AGREEMENT

Signature date: This Agreement is made on: _____ 2004

Parties: The parties to this Agreement (the 'Parties') are:

1. [**ABC Limited** ('ABC')] [a company incorporated in England and Wales] [registration number •] [whose registered office is at •]; and

2. [**XYZ, Inc.** ('XYZ')] [a US corporation incorporated in the State of Delaware] [whose principal place of business is at •].

Field and purpose: The Parties wish to hold discussions in the field of • (the 'Field'). XYZ wishes to receive confidential information in the Field from ABC for the purpose of considering whether to enter into a further agreement with ABC (the 'Permitted Purpose').

It is agreed as follows:

1.   Confidentiality obligations

1.1   In consideration of ABC providing Confidential Information, at its discretion, to XYZ, XYZ shall:

1.1.1   Keep the Confidential Information secret and confidential;

1.1.2   Neither disclose nor permit the disclosure of any Confidential Information to any person, except for disclosure to Authorised Persons in accordance with clause 2, or to a court or other public body in accordance with clause 3;

1.1.3   Not use the Confidential Information for any purpose, whether commercial or non-commercial, other than the Permitted Purpose;

1.1.4   [Make [no copies of the Confidential Information] [only such limited number of copies of the Confidential Information as are required for the Permitted Purpose, and provide those copies only to Authorised Persons];] and

1.1.5   Take proper and all reasonable measures to ensure the confidentiality of the Confidential Information.

1.2   For the purposes of this Agreement, the following words shall have the following meanings:

1.2.1   'Information' shall include information [whether of a technical, commercial or any other nature whatsoever] provided directly or indirectly by ABC to XYZ in oral or documentary form or by way of models, biological or chemical materials or other tangible form or by demonstrations and whether before, on or after the date of this Agreement.

1.2.2   'Confidential Information' shall mean:

1.2.2.1 in respect of Information provided in documentary form or by way of a model or in other tangible form, Information which at the time of provision is marked or otherwise designated to show expressly or by necessary implication that it is imparted in confidence; and

1.2.2.2 in respect of Information that is imparted orally, any information that ABC or its representatives informed XYZ at the time of disclosure was imparted in confidence; and

1.2.2.3 in respect of Confidential Information imparted orally, any note or record of the disclosure [and any evaluation materials prepared by XYZ that incorporate any Confidential Information]; and

1.2.2.4 any copy of any of the foregoing; and

1.2.2.5 [the fact that discussions are taking place between XYZ and ABC.]

2.   Disclosure to employees

2.1   XYZ may disclose the Confidential Information to those of its officers, employees [and professional advisers] (together, 'Authorised Persons') who:

2.1.1   reasonably need to receive the Confidential Information to enable XYZ to achieve the Permitted Purpose;

2.1.2   have been informed by XYZ (a) of the confidential nature of the Confidential Information and (b) that ABC provided the Confidential Information to XYZ subject to the provisions of a written confidentiality agreement;

2.1.3   [in the case of XYZ's officers and employees,] have [written] confidentiality obligations to XYZ that (a) are no less onerous than the provisions of this Agreement and (b) apply to the Confidential Information, and who have been instructed to treat the Confidential Information as confidential;

2.1.4   [in the case of XYZ's professional advisers] [other than its solicitors], [have been provided with a copy of this Agreement and] have agreed with XYZ in writing to comply with the obligations of XYZ under this Agreement, [and that agreement provides that ABC will be entitled to enforce the agreement as a third-party beneficiary]; and

2.1.5   [in the case of XYZ's solicitors, have confirmed that they will treat the Confidential Information as if it were XYZ's confidential information and therefore subject to the rules of the Law Society concerning client information.]

2.2   XYZ shall [be responsible for taking reasonable action to] ensure that its Authorised Persons comply with XYZ's obligations under this Agreement [and shall be liable to ABC for any breach of this Agreement by such Authorised Persons].

3.   Disclosure to court

To the extent that XYZ is required to disclose Confidential Information by order of a court or other public body that has jurisdiction over XYZ, it may do so. Before making such a disclosure XYZ shall, if the circumstances permit:

3.1   Inform ABC of the proposed disclosure as soon as possible (and if possible before the court or other public body orders the disclosure of the Confidential Information);

3.2   Ask the court or other public body to treat the Confidential Information as confidential; and

3.3   Permit ABC to make representations to the court or other public body in respect of the disclosure and/or confidential treatment of the Confidential Information.

4.   Exceptions to confidentiality obligations

XYZ's obligations under clause 2 shall not apply to Confidential Information that:

4.1   XYZ possessed before ABC disclosed it to XYZ;

4.2   Is or becomes publicly known, other than as a result of breach of the terms of this Agreement by XYZ or by anyone to whom XYZ disclosed it; [or]

4.3   XYZ obtains from a third party, and the third party was not under any obligation of confidentiality with respect to the Confidential Information; [or]

4.4   [Is developed by any of XYZ's employees who have not had any direct or indirect access to, or use or knowledge of, the ABC's Confidential Information.]

5.   Return of information and surviving obligations

5.1   Subject to clause 5.2, XYZ shall (a) at ABC's request, and also (b) upon any termination of this Agreement:

5.1.1   Return and provide to ABC all documents and other materials that contain any of the Confidential Information, including all copies made by XYZ representatives;

5.1.2   Permanently delete all electronic copies of Confidential Information from XYZ's computer systems; and

5.1.3   Provide to ABC a certificate, signed by an officer of XYZ, confirming that the obligations referred to in clauses 5.1.1 and 5.1.2 have been met.

5.2   As an exception to its obligations under clause 5.1, XYZ may retain one copy of the Confidential Information, in paper form, in XYZ's legal files for the purpose of ensuring compliance with XYZ's obligations under this Agreement.

5.3   Following the date of any termination of this Agreement, or any return of Confidential Information to ABC ('Final Date'), (a) XYZ shall make no further use of the Confidential Information, and (b) XYZ's obligations under this Agreement shall otherwise continue in force, in respect of Confidential Information disclosed prior to the Final Date, in each case [for a period of [1] [5] [10] [15] [20] years from the [date of this Agreement][Final Date]] [without limit of time].

6.   General

6.1   XYZ acknowledges and agrees that all property, including intellectual property, in the Confidential Information shall remain with and be vested in ABC.

6.2   This Agreement does not include, expressly or by implication, any representations, warranties or other obligations:

6.2.1 To grant XYZ any licence or rights other than as may be expressly stated in this Agreement;

6.2.2 To require ABC to disclose, continue disclosing or update any Confidential Information;

6.2.3 To require ABC to negotiate or continue negotiating with XYZ with respect to any further agreement, and either party may withdraw from such negotiations at any time without liability; nor

6.2.4 As to the accuracy, efficacy, completeness, capabilities, safety or any other qualities whatsoever of any information or materials provided under this Agreement.

6.3 The validity, construction and performance of this Agreement shall be governed by English law and shall be subject to the [non-]exclusive jurisdiction of the courts of England and Wales, to which the parties to this Agreement submit.

Agreed by the parties through their authorised signatories:

For and on behalf of
[ABC Limited]

For and on behalf of
[XYZ, Inc.]

_____

Signed

_____

Signed

_____

Name

_____

Name

_____

Title

_____

Title

B ROUTINE TWO-WAY CONFIDENTIALITY AGREEMENT

Signature date: This Agreement is made on: _____ 2004

Parties: The parties to this Agreement (the 'Parties') are:

1. [**ABC Limited** ('ABC')] [a company incorporated in England and Wales] [registration number •] [whose registered office is at •]; and

2. [**XYZ, Inc.** ('XYZ')] [a US corporation incorporated in the State of Delaware] [whose principal place of business is at •].

Field and purpose: The Parties wish to hold discussions in the field of • (the 'Field'). Each party wishes to receive confidential information in the Field from the other party for the purpose of considering whether to enter into a further agreement with the other party (the 'Permitted Purpose').

It is agreed as follows:

1.   Confidentiality obligations

1.1   In consideration of the Disclosing Party providing Confidential Information, at its discretion, to the Receiving Party, the Receiving Party shall:

1.1.1   Keep the Confidential Information secret and confidential;

1.1.2   Neither disclose nor permit the disclosure of any Confidential Information to any person, except for disclosure to Authorised Persons in accordance with clause 2, or to a court or other public body in accordance with clause 3;

1.1.3   Not use the Confidential Information for any purpose, whether commercial or non-commercial, other than the Permitted Purpose;

1.1.4   [Make [no copies of the Confidential Information] [only such limited number of copies of the Confidential Information as are required for the Permitted Purpose, and provide those copies only to Authorised Persons];] and

1.1.5   Take proper and all reasonable measures to ensure the confidentiality of the Confidential Information.

1.2   For the purposes of this Agreement, the following words shall have the following meanings:

1.2.1   'Information' shall include information [whether of a technical, commercial or any other nature whatsoever] provided directly or indirectly by the Disclosing Party to the Receiving Party in oral or documentary form or by way of models, biological or chemical materials or other tangible form or by demonstrations and whether before, on or after the date of this Agreement.

1.2.2 'Confidential Information' shall mean:

1.2.2.1 in respect of Information provided in documentary form or by way of a model or in other tangible form, Information which at the time of provision is marked or otherwise designated to show expressly or by necessary implication that it is imparted in confidence; and

1.2.2.2 in respect of Information that is imparted orally, any information that the Disclosing Party or its representatives informed the Receiving Party at the time of disclosure was imparted in confidence; and

1.2.2.3 in respect of Confidential Information imparted orally, any note or record of the disclosure [and any evaluation materials prepared by the Receiving Party that incorporate any Confidential Information]; and

1.2.2.4 any copy of any of the foregoing; and

1.2.2.5 [the fact that discussions are taking place between the Receiving Party and the Disclosing Party.]

1.2.3 'Disclosing Party' shall mean the party to this Agreement that discloses Information, directly or indirectly to the Receiving Party under or in anticipation of this Agreement.

1.2.4 'Receiving Party' shall mean the party to this Agreement that receives Information, directly or indirectly from the Disclosing Party.

2. Disclosure to employees

2.1 The Receiving Party may disclose the Confidential Information to those of its officers, employees [and professional advisers] (together, 'Authorised Persons') who:

2.1.1 reasonably need to receive the Confidential Information to enable the Receiving Party to achieve the Permitted Purpose;

2.1.2 have been informed by the Receiving Party (a) of the confidential nature of the Confidential Information and (b) that the Disclosing Party provided the Confidential Information to the Receiving Party subject to the provisions of a written confidentiality agreement;

2.1.3 [in the case of the Receiving Party's officers and employees,] have [written] confidentiality obligations to the Receiving Party that (a) are no less onerous than the provisions of this Agreement and

(b) apply to the Confidential Information, and who have been instructed to treat the Confidential Information as confidential;

2.1.4 [in the case of the Receiving Party's professional advisers] [other than its solicitors], [have been provided with a copy of this Agreement and] have agreed with the Receiving Party in writing to comply with the obligations of the Receiving Party under this Agreement, [and that agreement provides that the Disclosing Party will be entitled to enforce the agreement as a third-party beneficiary]; and

2.1.5 [in the case of the Receiving Party's solicitors, have confirmed that they will treat the Confidential Information as if it were the Receiving Party's confidential information and therefore subject to the rules of the Law Society concerning client information.]

2.2 The Receiving Party shall [be responsible for taking reasonable action to] ensure that its Authorised Persons comply with the Receiving Party's obligations under this Agreement [and shall be liable to the Disclosing Party for any breach of this Agreement by such Authorised Persons].

3. Disclosure to court

To the extent that the Receiving Party is required to disclose Confidential Information by order of a court or other public body that has jurisdiction over the Receiving Party, it may do so. Before making such a disclosure the Receiving Party shall, if the circumstances permit:

3.1 Inform the Disclosing Party of the proposed disclosure as soon as possible (and if possible before the court or other public body orders the disclosure of the Confidential Information);

3.2 Ask the court or other public body to treat the Confidential Information as confidential; and

3.3 Permit the Disclosing Party to make representations to the court or other public body in respect of the disclosure and/or confidential treatment of the Confidential Information.

4. Exceptions to confidentiality obligations

The Receiving Party's obligations under clause 2 shall not apply to Confidential Information that:

4.1 The Receiving Party possessed before the Disclosing Party disclosed it to the Receiving Party;

4.2   Is or becomes publicly known, other than as a result of breach of the terms of this Agreement by the Receiving Party or by anyone to whom the Receiving Party disclosed it; [or]

4.3   The Receiving Party obtains from a third-party, and the third-party was not under any obligation of confidentiality with respect to the Confidential Information; [or]

4.4   [Is developed by any of the Receiving Party's employees who have not had any direct or indirect access to, or use or knowledge of, the Disclosing Party's Confidential Information.]

5.   Return of information and surviving obligations

5.1   Subject to clause 5.2, the Receiving Party shall (a) at the Disclosing Party's request, and also (b) upon any termination of this Agreement:

5.1.1   Return and provide to the Disclosing Party all documents and other materials that contain any of the Confidential Information, including all copies made by the Receiving Party representatives;

5.1.2   Permanently delete all electronic copies of Confidential Information from the Receiving Party's computer systems; and

5.1.3   Provide to the Disclosing Party a certificate, signed by an officer of the Receiving Party, confirming that the obligations referred to in clauses 5.1.1 and 5.1.2 have been met.

5.2   As an exception to its obligations under clause 5.1, the Receiving Party may retain one copy of the Confidential Information, in paper form, in the Receiving Party's legal files for the purpose of ensuring compliance with the Receiving Party's obligations under this Agreement.

5.3   Following the date of any termination of this Agreement, or any return of Confidential Information to the Disclosing Party ('Final Date'), (a) the Receiving Party shall make no further use of the Confidential Information, and (b) the Receiving Party's obligations under this Agreement shall otherwise continue in force, in respect of Confidential Information disclosed prior to the Final Date, in each case [for a period of [1] [5] [10] [15] [20] years from the [date of this Agreement][Final Date]] [without limit of time].

6.   General

6.1   The Receiving Party acknowledges and agrees that all property, including intellectual property, in Confidential Information disclosed to it by the Disclosing Party shall remain with and be vested in the Disclosing Party.

6.2 This Agreement does not include, expressly or by implication, any representations, warranties or other obligations:

6.2.1 To grant the Receiving Party any licence or rights other than as may be expressly stated in this Agreement;

6.2.2 To require the Disclosing Party to disclose, continue disclosing or update any Confidential Information;

6.2.3 To require the Disclosing Party to negotiate or continue negotiating with the Receiving Party with respect to any further agreement, and either party may withdraw from such negotiations at any time without liability; nor

6.2.4 As to the accuracy, efficacy, completeness, capabilities, safety or any other qualities whatsoever of any information or materials provided under this Agreement.

6.3 The validity, construction and performance of this Agreement shall be governed by English law and shall be subject to the [non-]exclusive jurisdiction of the courts of England and Wales, to which the parties to this Agreement submit.

Agreed by the parties through their authorised signatories:

| **For and on behalf of** | **For and on behalf of** |
| **[ABC Limited]** | **[XYZ, Inc.]** |

| _____ | _____ |
| Signed | Signed |

| _____ | _____ |
| Name | Name |

| _____ | _____ |
| Title | Title |

C ADDITIONAL CLAUSES THAT MAY BE SUITABLE IN PARTICULAR SITUATIONS

1. XYZ undertakes to ABC that, for a period of 2 years from the date of this Agreement, it shall not, directly or indirectly, make any investment in, or otherwise be involved in controlling or managing, any company involved in developing new or improved products or processes relating to •, without the prior written consent of ABC.

2. ABC is not under any obligation to reimburse any costs and expenses which XYZ or its advisers may incur in connection with the discussions relating to the Permitted Purpose.

3. XYZ is acting in relation to the Permitted Purpose as principal and not as agent or broker for or in concert with any other person.

4. XYZ acknowledges and agrees that any breach of this Agreement could cause injury to ABC and damages would not be an adequate remedy. In the event of a breach or threatened breach by XYZ, ABC shall be entitled to [apply for] injunctive relief in any court of competent jurisdiction [and XYZ shall not oppose any such application]. XYZ shall indemnify ABC against all costs, claims, demands and liabilities arising directly or indirectly out of a breach. Nothing contained in this Agreement shall be construed as prohibiting ABC from pursuing any other remedies available to it for a breach or threatened breach.

5. If XYZ makes or observes any new discovery, improvement or invention ('Invention') relating to the Confidential Information [or as a direct result of the Project], it will bring this to the attention of ABC. Neither Party shall make or seek to make actual commercial gain from such an Invention, or make any patent application or secure any other proprietary rights to legally protect any such Invention, except with the prior written agreement of the other Party. ABC will, at all times, retain the right to use an Invention for non-commercial research purposes.

6. The Parties shall not arrange nor permit the publication of any information regarding the results or outcome of the Confidential Information without the prior written consent of the other Party, such consent shall not be unreasonably withheld.

7. XYZ acknowledges that the Information may include information, documents and other articles protected by the Official Secrets Acts 1911 and 1989 and will therefore require that the highest standards of confidentiality be maintained. Breach of the Official Secrets Acts is a criminal offence.

8. XYZ acknowledges that in addition to the terms of this Agreement it will be bound by the provisions of the Official Secrets Acts 1911 and 1989. In particular, XYZ acknowledges that:

    i.   disclosure of any Information relating to defence in breach of the terms of this Agreement may be a criminal offence; and

   ii.   failure to take such care to prevent unauthorised disclosure of any Information relating to defence as it might reasonably be expected to take is a criminal offence. By way of example, XYZ must take all practical steps to ensure that Information is secured and not accessible to third parties: for instance, by locking manual files away and by securing computer files and data.

9.   [*additional wording that could be inserted at end of clause 1.2.2.2 of Precedent A*], and that is also reduced to writing, marked 'Confidential' and sent to XYZ within 30 days of the original, oral disclosure.

10.   The information in this document is the property of •, and is to be held strictly in confidence by the recipient [subject to the terms of a confidentiality agreement between • and * dated [xxx]]. No copy is to be made without the written permission of •. The contents of this document © [*name of copyright owner*] [2003].

D EXTRA-STRONG CLAUSE TO BE ADDED TO STANDARD CDA

Without prejudice to the generality of the foregoing, the Receiving Party undertakes that, except as may be permitted in any future written agreement between the Parties:

(a) The Receiving Party shall not make any inventions or developments using or based on the Disclosing Party's Confidential Information, and if any such inventions or developments are made, the Receiving Party shall assign all rights in them to the Disclosing Party or its nominee;

(b) The Receiving Party shall not attempt to replicate the Disclosing Party's Confidential Information nor to investigate detailed aspects of the Disclosing Party's Confidential Information that were not disclosed by the Disclosing Party; and

(c) The Receiving Party shall not use the Disclosing Party's Confidential Information directly or indirectly to procure a commercial benefit to the Receiving Party or a commercial disbenefit to the Disclosing Party (including without limitation to support any patent applications being made by the Receiving Party or to obtain or submit evidence to support an allegation of patent infringement).

E CONFIDENTIALITY CLAUSE IN SETTLEMENT AGREEMENT

Except as expressly stated in this Settlement Agreement, XYZ and ABC shall each keep their dealings pursuant to the [*insert details of the agreement, if any, that is the subject of the dispute*] ('Prior Agreement') and this Settlement Agreement confidential and each of them shall not without the prior written consent of the other disclose, or permit the disclosure to any person of any details of the Prior Agreement or any matters connected with the Prior Agreement or the terms of this Settlement Agreement save:

1.1   as required by law or insofar as they are already public knowledge (except by reason of a breach by that Party of this Clause X); and

1.2   that ABC intends after the making of this Settlement Agreement to issue a Press Release in the agreed terms set out in Schedule • to this Settlement Agreement and the Parties may answer in terms consistent with and limited to the terms of that Press Release; and

1.3   that nothing in this clause shall prevent ABC from disclosing such information under obligations of confidentiality consistent with the terms of this Clause to its professional advisers [and shareholders].

F CONFIDENTIALITY CLAUSES IN CONTRACT OF EMPLOYMENT (TECHNOLOGY-BASED COMPANY)

In the course of your employment by the Company, you may acquire or develop confidential information concerning the technology, business or activities of the Company. You acknowledge that the Company's confidential information includes, without limitation, the following items unless these have been publicly disclosed by the Company:

(a) scientific and technical information, including details of research projects and plans, compounds under development, results and data from trials, and the skills, experience and qualifications of individuals working for the Company;

(b) commercial information, including the terms of commercial agreements (and the existence of such agreements), the identity of customers, suppliers and collaborative partners, and buying and selling policies and procedures;

(c) strategic and financial information, including business plans, Board decisions, past and current projects and proposals, and unpublished accounts; and

(d) third-party information, including confidential information relating to any Group Company and information received in confidence from a third party, including information provided by collaborative partners.

You undertake to be careful and diligent so as not to cause any unauthorised disclosure or use of the Company's confidential information. During your employment by the Company, and after you leave the Company, you undertake that you will not:

(a) disclose the Company's confidential information to any person; nor

(b) use the Company's confidential information other than for the purpose of the Company's business and as directed by the Company.

The obligations set out in clause • above shall not apply:

(a) where you are authorised to disclose or use the information by the Board of Directors of the Company;

(b) where you are ordered to disclose the information by a Court (provided that, if circumstances permit, you will inform the Company in advance of disclosure and apply to the Court to have the information treated as confidential by the Court);

(c) to information or knowledge which becomes available for use by the public generally, other than through your default; nor

(d) following termination of your employment, to information which becomes part of your professional skill and knowledge and which does not include any confidential information of the Company.

G CONFIDENTIALITY AGREEMENT WITH AUDITOR OF ROYALTIES

THIS AGREEMENT dated _____ is between:

1. [ABC] LTD ('[ABC]'), a company incorporated in England and Wales, whose principal place of business is at [ ]; and

2. [XYZ] [LTD] [PLC] (the 'Recipient') whose principal place of business is at [ ].

WHEREAS [ABC] is considering commissioning the Recipient to audit certain intellectual property licences and other agreements to which [ABC] is a party and to review related information; such agreements and information are confidential and the Recipient wishes to receive such information and [ABC] is willing to disclose it on the terms set out below.

IT IS AGREED AS FOLLOWS:

1. Definitions

In this Agreement, the following words shall have the following meanings:

'Information' Shall include information provided directly or indirectly by [ABC] (or by parties with whom [ABC] has a contractual or other relationship and whose activities are being or to be audited on [ABC]'s behalf) to the Recipient in oral or documentary form or by way of models, biological or chemical materials or other tangible form or by demonstrations and whether before, on or after the date of this Agreement. 'Information' includes without limitation both scientific and commercial information, including business ideas and plans.

'Confidential Information' Shall mean:
   (a) in respect of Information provided in documentary form or by way of a model or in other tangible form, Information which at the time of provision is marked or otherwise designated to show expressly or by necessary implication that it is imparted in confidence;
   (b) in respect of Information that is imparted orally, any information that [ABC] or its representatives informed the Recipient or its representatives at the time of disclosure was imparted in confidence;

107

(c)   in respect of Confidential Information imparted orally, any note or record of the disclosure;

(d)   any copy of any of the foregoing; and

(e)   the fact that discussions are taking place between [ABC] and the Recipient.

'Permitted Purpose'   Shall mean that the Confidential Information may only be used by the Recipient for the purpose of advising [ABC] in relation to agreements to which [ABC] is a party.

2.   Undertakings

2.1   In consideration of the provision of Confidential Information by [ABC] or at its request to the Recipient and the sum of £1 now paid to the Recipient, receipt of which it acknowledges, the Recipient undertakes:

(a)   to keep the Confidential Information secret at all times;

(b)   not to disclose it or allow it to be disclosed in whole or in part to any third party without [ABC]'s prior written consent; and

(c)   not to use it in whole or in part for any purpose except for the Permitted Purpose.

2.2   The Recipient further undertakes to take proper and all reasonable measures to ensure the confidentiality of the Confidential Information.

2.3   The Recipient also undertakes to enter into any confidentiality agreement reasonably required by any other party being audited by the Recipient on [ABC]'s behalf, including without limitation licensees and collaborative partners of [ABC].

3.   Exceptions

The obligations of confidentiality set out in this Agreement shall not apply to any Information that the Recipient can show by written records:

(a)   was known to the Recipient before the Information was imparted by [ABC], or is in or subsequently comes into the public domain (through no fault on the Recipient's part);

(b)   is received by the Recipient without restriction on disclosure or use from a third party lawfully entitled to make the disclosure to the Recipient without such restrictions; or

(c)   is developed by any of the Recipient's employees who have not had any direct or indirect access to, or use or knowledge of, the Information imparted by [ABC] or at its request.

4.   Disclosure to employees

4.1   The Recipient undertakes to permit access to the Confidential Information only to those of its directors and employees who reasonably need access to such Confidential Information for the Permitted Purpose, and on the conditions that such directors and employees shall have:

(a)   entered into legally binding confidentiality obligations to the Recipient on terms equivalent to those set out in this Agreement (and such obligations extend to the Confidential Information);

(b)   been informed of [ABC]'s interest in the Confidential Information and the terms of this Agreement, and instructed to treat the Confidential Information as secret and confidential in accordance with the provisions of this Agreement.

4.2   The Recipient shall be responsible for ensuring that its directors and employees comply with the provisions of this Agreement.

5.   Return of information and property

5.1   The Recipient acknowledges and agrees that the property and copyright in the Confidential Information, including any documents, files and other items, including copies, containing any Confidential Information, belongs to [ABC].

5.2   At [ABC]'s written request, the Recipient will return immediately to [ABC] all Confidential Information which the Recipient received under this Agreement and which may still be in the Recipient's possession, including any copies made, and the Recipient will make no further use or disclosure of any of it.

5.3   The Recipient may, however, keep one copy of the Confidential Information in the Recipient's legal adviser's files solely for the purpose of enabling the Recipient to comply with the provisions of this Agreement.

5.4   The obligations on the Recipient under this Agreement shall continue in force for a period of 15 years from the date of this Agreement.

6. No implied rights

6.1 This Agreement shall not be construed:

    (a) to grant the Recipient any licence or rights other than as expressly set out herein in respect of the Confidential Information; nor

    (b) to require [ABC] to disclose any Confidential Information to the Recipient.

6.2 No warranty or representation, express or implied, is given as to the accuracy, efficacy, completeness, capabilities or safety of any materials or information provided under this Agreement.

7. Law and jurisdiction

This Agreement shall be governed by and construed in accordance with English law and shall be subject to the non-exclusive jurisdiction of the English courts.

For and on behalf of
[ABC] LIMITED

For and on behalf of
[Recipient] [LIMITED] [PLC]

Signed: _____

Signed: _____

Print name: _____

Print name: _____

Title: _____

Title: _____

Date: _____

Date: _____

H VERY SHORT AND SIMPLE ONE-WAY CONFIDENTIALITY AGREEMENT (NOT FOR USE WHERE INFORMATION IS VALUABLE)

Dear •

We refer to the discussions between [ABC Limited ('ABC')] and [XYZ, Inc. ('XYZ')] relating to • (the 'Proposed Agreement'). XYZ has requested certain confidential information concerning ABC. In consideration of ABC agreeing to disclose certain of its confidential information to XYZ, XYZ agrees as follows.

1. In this letter agreement, 'Confidential Information' means any or all information whether disclosed in written, electronic, oral or other form, whether in connection with the Proposed Agreement or the general business of ABC or otherwise, which is disclosed by ABC to XYZ or otherwise obtained from ABC, but excluding information which:

    (a) was already known to XYZ;

    (b) was already public knowledge on the date of its disclosure by ABC to XYZ;

    (c) subsequently becomes public knowledge through no fault on XYZ's part; or

    (d) is received by XYZ from a third party who has the lawful right to disclose it to XYZ without imposing obligations of confidentiality upon XYZ.

2. XYZ shall, and shall ensure that its employees shall:

    (a) hold the Confidential Information in confidence, taking all reasonable security precautions for its protection;

    (b) not disclose it whether in whole or in part to a third party;

    (c) use it only for the purpose of evaluating whether it wishes to enter into the Proposed Agreement with ABC; and

    (d) not copy it without the prior written consent of ABC.

3. At the request of ABC, XYZ shall immediately return the Confidential Information and any copies made of it and shall make no further use or disclosure of them. All documents and other materials provided by ABC to XYZ containing Confidential Information and all copies of them shall at all times be and be deemed to be the property of ABC. If at any time XYZ shall decide that it does not wish to enter into the Proposed Agreement, all Confidential Information in its possession shall be returned forthwith to ABC.

111

4.   This letter agreement shall continue in force until the date on which **XYZ** notifies **ABC** that it no longer wishes to receive ABC's Confidential Information and shall then terminate. Thereafter the obligations set out in this Agreement shall continue in respect of Confidential Information disclosed prior to such termination date [without limit of time][for a period of • years from the date of this letter agreement].

5.   This letter agreement is made under English law and the parties submit to the [non-]exclusive jurisdiction of the English courts.

Yours faithfully

For and on behalf of [ABC Limited]   Agreed for and on behalf of [XYZ, Inc.]

_____   _____

Signed   Signed

_____   _____

Date   Date

I LETTER CERTIFYING DESTRUCTION OF CONFIDENTIAL INFORMATION

[date]

[disclosing party's name and address]

For the attention of [   ]

Dear Sirs

Confidentiality agreement between [   ] (the 'Recipient') and [   ] ('Disclosing Party') dated [   ] ('Confidentiality Agreement')

I refer to the documentation and other materials and information that the Disclosing Party has provided to the Recipient under the Confidentiality Agreement, including all copies and extracts made by the Recipient, and whether recorded on paper, tape, disk (internal or external) or any other medium (together, the 'Disclosing Party Property').

I hereby certify as an officer of the Recipient that:

1. All of the Disclosing Party Property has been destroyed or returned to the Disclosing Party; and
2. The Recipient has not retained the whole or any part of the Disclosing Party Property in any medium, including without limitation on any computer system, storage device or back-up facility, and an appropriately qualified representative of the Recipient has diligently checked that this is the case; and
3. The Recipient shall not in the future make use of, nor disclose to any person, any of the Disclosing Party Property.

Certified by, for and on behalf of the Recipient by a Director or Company Secretary:

_____

signed

_____

print name

_____

title

_____

date

J CONFIDENTIALITY UNDERTAKING BY RESEARCHER TO A THIRD PARTY COMPANY

To: [   ] Limited (the 'Company')
       [address]

[name of institution] (the 'Institution') has entered into a contract with the Company dated [   ] (the 'Agreement').

I [name] of [address], acknowledge that:

(a) the Institution will receive and generate confidential information under the Agreement in respect of which it will have confidentiality obligations to the Company [including information relating to [   ] (the 'Product')]; and

(b) that I may gain access to or be involved in generating such confidential information, and accordingly I agree to be bound by confidentiality obligations to the Company as set out in this letter.

I confirm and agree as follows:

1.   In this letter, 'Company Confidential Information' means all information relating to [the Product], business affairs or finances of the Company, and includes without limitation all information related to:

     (a) any Company intellectual property; and

     (b) any intellectual property created, conceived or reduced to practice under the Agreement (including any improvements, modifications, enhancements and adaptations of any part of the Company intellectual property) ('Agreement IP').

2.   I undertake to:

     (a) use the Company Confidential Information only in the performance of services under the terms of the Agreement and not for any other purpose whatsoever;

     (b) keep the Company Confidential Information confidential and not directly or indirectly to disclose or permit to be disclosed, to make available or permit to be made available the same to any third party or to any other employee or research associate of the Institution who is not directly involved in the provision of the services under the terms of the Agreement; and

     (c) keep the Company Confidential Information separate at all times from other confidential information within my possession or control and to ensure that it remains at all times the sole property of the Company.

3. I undertake and acknowledge that under the terms of the Agreement, the Institution is required promptly to disclose to the Company any and all Agreement IP and that all right, title and interest in such Agreement IP shall vest in and be assigned to the Company. I confirm and acknowledge that I shall have no right, title or interest whatsoever in all or any part of the Agreement IP and I confirm and acknowledge that all right, title and interest in any part of the Agreement IP identified, conceived, reduced to practice or created by me in the performance of the services under the terms of the Agreement, shall vest absolutely in the Institution as the sole owner thereof.

Executed and delivered as a Deed   **Witnessed by:**
by [name] upon signature

_____
signed

_____
signature

_____
print name

_____
date

_____
address

Index

Design Law

Protecting and Exploiting Rights

Margaret Briffa and
Lee Gage

This practical new book guides
practitioners through the fast
changing and increasingly complex
area of design law. It clearly outlines
each of the different types of design
protection, demonstrating how best
to exploit designs to their full
commercial potential and guard rights against infringement.

The book highlights the factors that need to be considered when
selecting an appropriate method of design protection and offers
practical advice on how to set about obtaining and enforcing rights.

More current than any other work on the subject, the authors
provide authoritative notes on the latest law and cases.

The practical nature of the book is enhanced by case studies,
examples of good and bad practice, workflow diagrams, checklists,
and relevant statutory materials and precedents.

Available from Marston Book Services:
Tel. 01235 465 656.

1 85328 817 9
448 pages
£59.95
2004

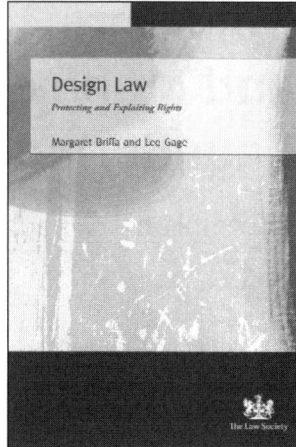

The Law Society

Solicitors and Money Laundering

A Compliance Handbook

Peter Camp

This authoritative handbook clearly demonstrates how the new anti-money laundering laws apply to solicitor's practices. It highlights areas of practice most at risk and gives practical advice on how to introduce anti-money laundering procedures enabling firms to recognise and report suspicious transactions.

The practical nature of the book is enhanced by helpful precedents, guidance material and statutory material, including:

- a precedent money laundering manual
- client identification form, internal reporting form and NCIS reporting forms
- official NCIS guidance on reporting suspicious transactions.

Written by a recognised expert, taking account of the latest Law Society guidelines it is essential reading for solicitors and their professional advisers looking to meet compliance objectives.

Available from Marston Book Services:
Tel. 01235 465 656.

1 85328 920 5
288 pages
£49.95
Sept. 2004

The Law Society